THE MAGIC WORLD OF THE AMAZING RANDI

THE MAGIC WORLD OF THE AMAZING RANDI

by
James (The Amazing) Randi

Bob Adams, Inc., Holbrook, MA

ISBN: 1-55850-982-8

Published by
BOB ADAMS, INC.
P U B L I S H E R S
260 Center St., Holbrook, MA 02343

Printed in the United States of America.

10   9   8   7   6   5   4   3   2   1

ABOUT THE AUTHOR

James (The Amazing) Randi is one of the world's most respected authorities on magic and the claims of self-described psychics and paranormalists. Randi received the rare honor of being inducted into the Magician's Hall of Fame, and is a recipient of the MacArthur Foundation's Genius Award. He is the author of *Flim-Flam!*, *The Truth About Uri Geller*, and *Houdini: His Life and Art*.

DEDICATION

To my good friend, artist Jose Luis Alvarez, who has suffered through endless performances of the tricks in this book. His patience as I tested illusions on him warrants a medal.

ACKNOWLEDGMENTS

I express my gratitude here to the magicians from around the world who agreed to be represented here. By contributing some of their favorite tricks to The Wizard who holds this book, these artists have shown their willingness to share the joy of Magic.

Artist Penny Alexander prepared the illustrations that so clearly bring forth the performers and their miracles; with the help and advice of her husband, David (an experienced magician himself), Penny completed her excellent drawings on schedule and exactly as requested.

My editors managed to correct my grammatical errors and occasionally awkward use of English; they must not be forgotten.

Finally, I must note that Harry Smith, Johnny Giordemaine, Sid Lorraine, and the immortal Harry Blackstone Sr. started me in my profession; I cannot fail to thank them here for their kindness and love.

CONTENTS

INTRODUCTION

From beyond the misty centuries and the hidden chronicles of the ancients, with a sweeping bow, a wave of the wand, and open arms, I welcome you to the wonderful, exciting world of Magic!

You are about to enter a strange universe in which things are not as they seem, where the laws of Nature are suspended by Wizards who hold the keys to certain mysteries. Here, we will find wonders of the mind and quick-fingered miracles that defy detection. And *you* will be able to master these sorceries!

In this book, I will describe for you some of the closely-guarded secrets of my art that will enable *you* to become a magician, too. Of course, you won't be sawing pretty ladies in half as David Copperfield has done, and unlike Harry Blackstone, you won't make an elephant vanish. Not for a while, anyway. And, I hope, you won't be escaping from a locked prison cell, as I have done so many times in my career. Those feats are only for the top professional magicians, and take many years of work and practice to perfect.

Professionals in Magic always start out as amateurs. Remember that a young lad named Erich Weiss began his interest in Magic after reading a book by a famous French performer named

Eugene Robert Houdin. Years later, having changed his name by borrowing part of that performer's name, he became Harry Houdini, the greatest escape artist who ever lived.

Though most people only want to learn basic tricks as a hobby and will always remain amateurs, maybe — just maybe — a reader of this book will develop an interest in the art of Magic and become skilled enough to earn a living as a Wizard.

So that you will understand how others became interested in this art, I will tell you a little about the lives of those who have agreed to share some secrets with you in this book. I have found that magicians are usually very generous in this respect. You can return that kindness by keeping the secrets you will learn here.

The routines I will describe can be performed by almost everybody. Some of the tricks need only a short period of practice, while others require many hours of repetition before they are mastered. Please wait until you are *very familiar* with how these tricks are done before you entertain your family and friends with them.

You will learn by reading this book carefully that there are a few rules all successful magicians follow. The most important rule is: make sure you are in charge of what's happening. It's *your* show, so stay in control. Don't be in a hurry to reveal the surprise at the end of your trick. Build some excitement. At the real "moment of truth," when the actual trickery takes place — an event that your audience should not suspect! — don't tense up.

Remember, too, that the magician is not a smart aleck who wants to show that he or she is smarter or quicker than The Spectator. You won't make many friends that way. The intent of the performer in Magic is to *entertain* people, to make them laugh, to mystify them. The reward should be the smiles and applause you receive. If, at the same time, you are paid for your performance, it's all the better!

Many of the leading show business personalities of our time were involved in Magic at one time. Harry Anderson, who delights us all on television with his comedy series, *Night Court*, began his career as a magician, and still performs the art of Magic whenever he can. Johnny Carson, who has featured many magicians on his famous *Tonight Show*, was once known as The Great Carsoni, and has never lost his love for the magical art. Well-known actor Jimmy Stewart was at one time an assistant to his good friend, magician Bill Neff. Talk show host and TV intellectual Dick Cavett still has an active interest in Magic, and learns new tricks at every opportunity.

Sad to say, there are some people who make their living by using trickery and telling the public that what they do is supernatural. Fortune-tellers, psychics, and other flim-flam artists prey upon innocent victims by pretending that they can predict the future, read minds, change events, or even heal the sick. They use some of the methods described in this book, though you may not recognize them.

We should reject this deception if it is not presented as entertainment. All of the magicians I will tell you about in these pages agree with me on that subject.

After you become familiar with how to do some of these tricks, you may wish to graduate to other levels of performance. At the end of the book you will find information on how to do just that. There are professional and semi-professional performers who are very willing to help beginners. And remember this — some of the best artists in Magic are amateurs! Magic is ideal as a hobby for people of all ages.

As I assembled this collection, I realized once again that there are very few female magicians. But make no mistake — those assistants you see carrying props about the stage for the magician are often just as skilled as the one who takes all the applause, and they too are responsible for the success of the act. There *are* very accomplished women who have made a success of magic. Diane Zimmerman, who performs today, and the great Cleopatra, in the past, are examples.

When I refer here to The Wizard, I mean *you,* and use "he" and "him" freely — but please remember that it could just as well be "she" and "her," as well. And, while we're on the subject, I have the hope that someday I will see a female magician sawing a male assistant into a few pieces! Isn't it about time? The person for whom you will be performing is called The Spectator. Let's hope you will always have a happy Spectator.

Let us begin! As I open the curtain and take you behind the scenes, you should know that Magic is an art that goes back thousands of years in time to the temples of ancient Egypt and Greece, to the high mountains of India and the palaces of the Orient. We had magicians among us even before we invented writing. And who knows? *You* may be so enthralled with this mystical, hidden art, that some day you, too, will sit down and write *your* book to introduce others to Magic. You may even begin your book by saying, "From beyond the misty centuries and the hidden chronicles of the ancients, with a sweeping bow, a wave of the wand, and open arms, I welcome you . . ."

James "The Amazing" Randi

Entering the Magic World . . .

JOAQUIN AYALA
Mexico

A few years ago, in Mexico, I met Mr. Joaquin Ayala. His refreshing stage act employed props of all kinds, including a silver flute, hundreds of playing cards fluttering down from above, and a huge pigeon that seemed to appear from nowhere, along with dozens of white doves. Sometime after that dazzling evening, I learned he'd developed an act in which he dressed like Mozart and used music written by that great composer.

It was not long before Joaquin was one of the leading magicians in Mexico, and he is now widely acclaimed in other countries as well. With his pretty wife Lilia, he travels all around the world, entertaining in night clubs and theatres.

Joaquin's contribution serves as a perfect first illusion in your repertoire as a Wizard! It's a cunning trick, in which a playing card is located and named by The Wizard . . . after it has been secretly selected by The Spectator. Like many such tricks, it uses the very simplest of methods with excellent results. An old-timer named Joe Kara first showed me something quite similar to this one when I was just sixteen years old. At that time, I was working for his Ten-In-One tent show, part of a carnival held during a summer holiday in Canada's eastern provinces.

Joe once told me that all he needed to work miracles was "a deck of cards and a little spit." And you know, I think he was probably right!

Actually, the secret method used to perform this trick is a familiar technique among professional card cheats. It is simple, easy to execute, and very effective. There are other methods similar to this idea that are also used by card cheats. I think you'd better settle for this one, though — I don't want you getting into trouble!

NICK NACK
THE EFFECT:

The Spectator is asked by The Wizard to shuffle a deck of cards, then divide it into three approximately equal piles, face down, side-by-side on the table. Of course, no one knows what cards are on the top of each of the three piles.   The Spectator is then to pick up the top card on any one of the three piles, look at it secretly and memorize it, then replace it, still face down, atop any of the three piles.

Now The Wizard discusses with The Spectator several of the options he had when choosing and replacing his chosen card. He then asks The Spectator to re-assemble the deck in any order, then cut the deck several times.

Up to now, The Wizard has not had the deck in his hands. At this point, though, he picks it up and cuts it a few times himself, then announces that he will make the secretly chosen card appear on top of the deck when it is named.

The Spectator names the secret card and then picks it off the top of the deck. There it is!

HOW IT'S DONE:

The problem is obvious. Before the deck is re-assembled, the Wizard knows *where* the card is, but does not know *what* it is, so it is necessary to identify it in some way.

One simple move by The Wizard does it all. The easiest way to identify the card would be to draw an "X" on the back, or turn it over and peek at it. Obviously, The Wizard has to be a bit more clever than that! Here's what he does. Just after The Spectator has replaced his card atop one of the piles, The Wizard gives him a short description of a few of the possible things he *might* have done. "You could have taken a card from here, looked at it, and replaced it here," he says, pointing at the piles as he speaks and lightly touching the backs of the cards. "But you chose to take a card from *here*," he says as he touches the place from where The Spectator took his card, "and you replaced it over here." At that point, The Wizard brings his hand down *on the back of The Spectator's card* and performs the secret move.

This is done with the thumb-nail (see illustration A). As The Wizard's fingers touch The Spectator's card, the fingers draw back the top card (that's the one we want to identify!) about a sixteenth of an inch — a very tiny bit. Now the card is hanging over the pile a little, and the thumb-nail presses into the edge of the card, about the center, enough to cut into the card's edge. Personally, I like to "slice" my thumb-nail down across the edge, to cut it easily, rather than pressing it into the edge.

The selected card is now marked. But The Spectator doesn't know that! Drawing his hand away, The Wizard immediately invites The Spectator to re-assemble the three piles in any order and cut the cards a few times, "to lose the card in the deck." True, the card *is* lost, but cutting the deck merely moves it around. It can now be found easily by The Wizard, no matter how often the deck is cut.

Picking up the deck, The Wizard cuts it a few times himself, at the same time looking at the end of the deck where the thumb-nail nick was made. The mark will stand out very well, and The Wizard will have no problem finding it. (See illustration B.) It is an easy matter now to cut the deck just above that mark, complete the cut, and place the deck face-down on the table. A glance at the edge of the top card will verify that it is The Spectator's card.

Now that the trick is actually accomplished, The Wizard can concentrate on building up to the climax. He announces that he will cause The Spectator's unknown card to rise to the top of the deck! Passing his hands over the deck a few times and mumbling a few appropriate "magical" words, he invites The Spectator to name his card out loud. Merely pointing at the top card, he confidently asks The Spectator to look at it.

As with all tricks in which you can use a borrowed "prop," it is better to do this with someone else's deck of cards. The deck must also be in good condition. Otherwise, there might be so many other nicks in the cards that things could get confusing!

After doing this trick, you should zip your thumb up and down the edge of the pack to "heal" the small mark you've made. This way, the evidence is erased, and, if you wish, you can use the pack for other tricks.

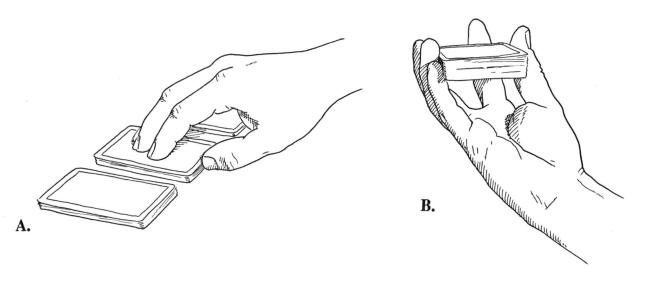

A.

B.

DAVID COPPERFIELD
U.S.A.

David Copperfield is one of the all-time great magic stars. His romantic, poetic approach to his art has set a style that many other artists have envied and even tried to imitate. When he made a jet plane vanish on television in 1982, everyone sat up and took notice. Then, a year later, he topped himself by making the Statue of Liberty fade away before an audience of millions of TV viewers!

David started studying magic at an early age. The Society of American Magicians accepted him as a full professional member — their youngest member ever — while he was in his teens. He even taught magic at New York University before he was twenty years old. Because of his extensive exposure on TV, he has probably been seen by more people than any other magician in history.

As an entertainer, Mr. Copperfield sings, dances, acts, and of course performs his wonderful magic around the world. His live theater show is a great thrill. Although he has received acclaim for his magical feats, he is proudest of his work for "Project Magic," a rehabilitative program that he designed for disabled people. Learning simple magic tricks can bring back motor skills and dexterity to those who have suffered injuries that limit their abilities. David believes that learning magic can also build a patient's self-esteem, and some 500 hospitals around the world are using his ideas for that very purpose.

David has offered to share with you an easily mastered "Project Magic" trick that seems to defy the laws of physics. You can always be ready to do this little puzzler, since all you'll need is an ordinary rubber band and a little practice.

THE JUMPING RUBBER BAND
THE EFFECT:

The Wizard clearly places a rubber band over the first and second fingers of his left hand, as shown in illustration A. The Wizard shows both sides of his hand. Now he closes all his fingers, and again shows both sides of his hand, then straightens out the four fingers again. A snapping noise is heard, and instantly, The Spectator sees that the rubber band is now located around *the other two fingers*!

There can't be a simpler effect than that, can there? It's just not possible for a rubber band to jump instantly off two fingers and land on two other fingers, but it has just happened!

HOW IT'S DONE:

First, choose a rubber band that will just fit around your two fingers. Make sure that The Spectator clearly sees how you have placed the band around the first two fingers of your left hand. Let him see both sides of your hand. Snap the rubber band a few times by pinching it and letting it go against your fingers to show The Spectator that it really is around your first two fingers.

Then, holding your left hand up with your palm toward you, reach up with your right hand to the part of the band that is on your first finger, and pinch the band between the right thumb and first finger of your right hand. Pull the band toward yourself, about an inch, stretching it over to the right a bit and making a triangular loop. (See illustration B.)

As you begin to curl all four fingers of your left hand, preparing to "make a fist," you insert the first two fingers of your left hand *into* the loop, which is now across the top edge of your fingernails. (See illustration C.) Pull the loop to the right so that it pops over the other two fingernails as well. Release the band, and from where you see it, your hand will look like illustration D.

The Spectator, watching your hand from the other side, can only see the rubber band passing around the first two fingers. Close your left thumb tightly against the side of your first finger to hide the place where the band goes over your fingernail, and press all your fingernails into your palm so the band cannot be seen there. (See illustration E.) Turn your fist to show The Spectator both sides of your hand. Snap the band once, as you did before. This reminds The Spectator that you did the same thing previously, when you first put the band on your two fingers.

Here's the big moment. The Spectator has seen you position the rubber band, and is convinced that it's "locked" in place by your fist. (See illustration F.) As you suddenly straighten out your fingers, the band seems to jump to the other two fingers! (See illustration G.) Again, offer your hand for close examination. Nothing suspicious can be seen!

I think that after you master this trick, you'll carry a rubber band around in your pocket at all times!

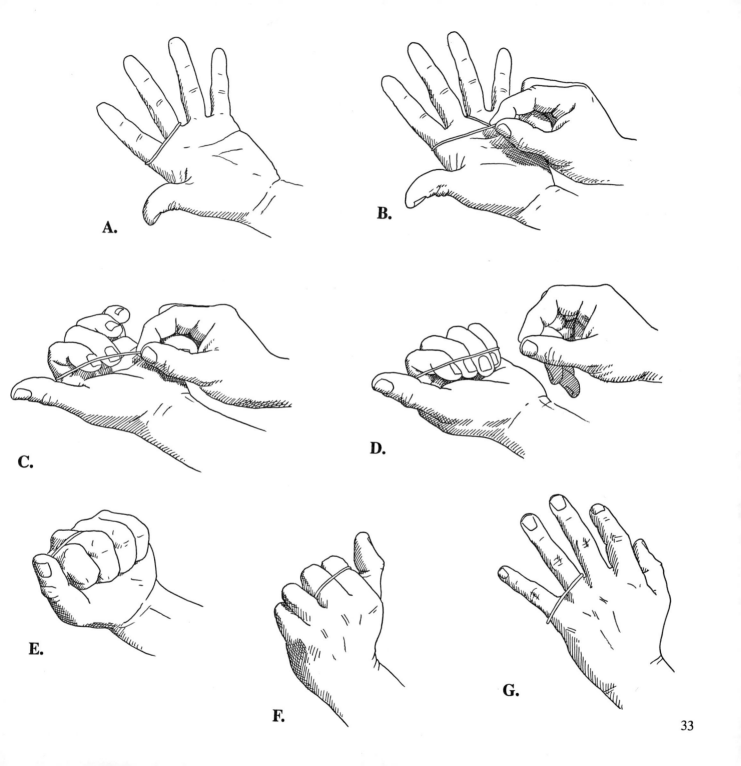

A.

B.

C.

D.

E.

F.

G.

33

ALAN NGUYEN
Viet Nam

Some years ago, while I was working in Washington, D.C., I ran into a young chap who was "working tables" in a restaurant. He was going about from table to table, entertaining the patrons while they waited for their food to arrive. It is not an easy task to dodge waiters who could trickle soup on a careless magician who isn't moving fast enough! But Alan Nguyen was quick with his hands and his feet, and he made a big impression on his fans.

Table work is a very specialized endeavor. Alan had to carry all his "props" in a small bag and could not take much room at the table, of course. He used everything in sight, from salt shakers to paper napkins, to work his miracles.

At an early age, Alan's family moved to San Francisco from Monterey, California, and he became fascinated by the conjurors there who work in the streets as entertainers. His parents, Chinese and Vietnamese immigrants, are very happy that their son is working as a magician.

First working the streets of Washington, then as an assistant to the magic team of Denny Lee & Minh, (whom you will also meet in this book), Alan gained a lot of stage magic knowledge. Now he bills himself as a "Genuine Oriental Illusionist," so that he will not be confused with the many magicians who adopt oriental costumes to look as if they came from the East.

Here is Alan's contribution to this book, and his special gift to you as a fellow conjuror. You'll do this trick while seated at a table. You only need a borrowed quarter, a salt-shaker (a straight-sided one is best), and two paper napkins.

THE TURNOVER COIN
THE EFFECT:

The Wizard places a quarter face down on the table, then covers it with a salt-shaker, which is in turn covered tightly with a paper napkin, then covered with a second napkin. The Wizard announces that he will now cause the coin to flip over while it is covered. The Spectator is allowed to see the coin one more time, checking that it is face-down. The Wizard then presses down on the covered salt-shaker. Instead of the coin turning over, however, the salt-shaker suddenly vanishes, and is re-produced from inside The Wizard's jacket pocket!

This trick incorporates all of the major effects you'll have to learn as a magician. It is a fine illusion. The Spectator expects to see the coin turn over, yet something very different occurs — taking The Spectator completely by surprise.

HOW IT'S DONE:

You should be wearing a jacket. The Spectator should be seated on the opposite side of the table. Place the coin deliberately, heads down, on the table about ten inches away from the table edge nearest you. Tell The Spectator that you will be able to cause the quarter to turn over, so that the coin will be heads up. Keep The Spectator's attention on the coin. Carefully place the salt-shaker on top of the coin (see illustration A) and tell The Spectator that it is now impossible for you to turn over the coin without being detected. "To make it even more difficult," you say, "I will also hide the coin from sight!" At this point, you unfold a paper napkin and spread it over the shaker, molding the paper to show the shape of the shaker. (See illustration B). Immediately, reach for a *second* paper napkin, and shape it tightly around the shaker so that the napkins will hold the shape of the shaker even if it's not there.

By now, The Spectator has become a little nervous about that coin. You look up and say, "I guess you wonder if I've done something tricky with that coin. Let's check and see if it's alright." You lift the paper napkins and the shaker off the coin, pushing it slightly forward toward The Spectator to show that the heads side is still face down. (See illustration C.)

"When you next see that coin," you pronounce, "it will be face-up!" You carefully replace the salt-shaker-plus-napkins on top of the coin. OR SO IT APPEARS! Actually, when showing the coin, you push it forward toward The Spectator with your left hand, and draw the napkins (with the shaker inside) toward the edge of the table. This move is done at the same speed as you have done all the other moves, so it looks unsuspicious. Just as the salt-shaker is clear of the table edge, you relax your hand and allow the shaker to slide out of the paper napkins. (See illustration C, again.) You don't allow the shaker shape of the napkins to collapse, of course, because you want it to appear as if the shaker is still under the napkins.

At the same speed, you now re-cover the coin by bringing the paper napkins back into position over the coin. However, there is no salt-shaker under the napkins, a fact unknown to The Spectator. If you carefully remove your hand, the napkins will rest atop the coin, looking as if the shaker is still there. (See illustration D.) Bring your right hand over the little "tent" of paper, rest it carefully atop the shaker-that-isn't-there, and suddenly press your hand down. The shaker has dissolved! (See illustration E.)

Uncover the coin, pick it up, and remark, "You know, that trick *always* goes wrong!" Crumple up the paper napkins, put them aside, throw your hands up in dismay, and drop both hands into your lap. With your right hand, take hold of the salt-shaker in your lap, and hold it as shown in illustration F. With your left hand, pull the left edge of your jacket away as if you are going to reach into your shirt pocket. Look down into the jacket and with your right hand reach into your inside jacket pocket, which supposedly contains the shaker. Keep the back of your hand toward The Spectator, so he cannot see the shaker. (See illustration G.) Immediately drop the shaker inside your pocket, then in the same move, pick it up again and pull it out of your jacket. Place the shaker on the table. Your illusion is complete.

People will talk about this trick for a long, long time. But — never repeat it for the same person, because anyone who has seen it will expect the shaker to disappear, and may catch you!

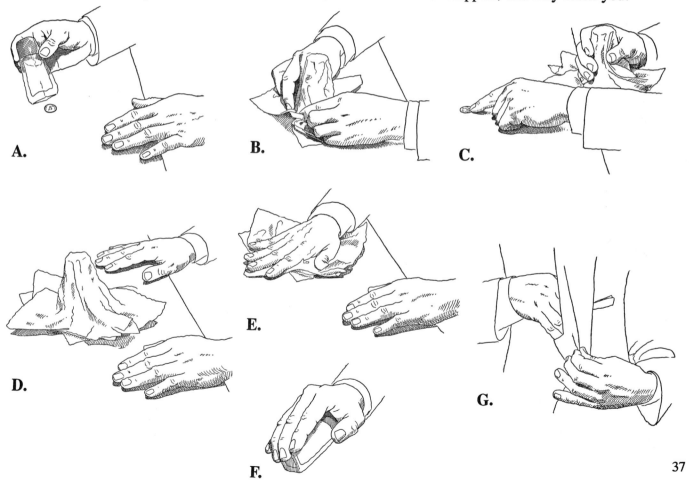

A.

B.

C.

D.

E.

F.

G.

OLEG MEDVEDEV
U.S.S.R.

It's interesting to note that although magicians from different parts of the world may look and dress differently, there are many things that they share with regard to personality and technique. I have traveled all over the world, and I've certainly found that to be true. One young magician I met was Oleg Medvedev, who lives in Russia. He charmed us all in Puerto Rico recently, when he attended a congress of young magicians. His bouncy, cheerful style and disposition won him many new friends.

Oleg has been active in magic since the age of seven. His first magic lessons came from his father, his sister Katya, and Vladimir Rudnev, president of the Moscow Magicians Club. Oleg and his sister took the second and third prizes, respectively, in small magic at the 1987 All-Union Magic Competition. On his own, Oleg took the second prize in manipulation in the sixteen-and-under age group.

This young performer works his act with billiard balls, coins, silk handkerchiefs, and lengths of rope. He moves about the stage very quickly, flashing a big smile as objects appear, change color, and disappear in his hands. Oleg has a very classical look about him, and he speaks English rather well. Many are predicting that he will be a successful professional performer some day very soon.

Magician Medvedev asked me to describe this very puzzling trick for you. All it requires is a simple shoelace and a handkerchief.

VANISHING KNOT, IS IT NOT?

THE EFFECT:

The Wizard shows a shoelace that has a simple, loose, overhand knot in it; the two ends of the shoelace have been tied together securely into a loop, using a complicated knot, as shown in illustration A. The ends of the shoelace protrude about two inches from the secure knot. The Wizard claims that he can *untie* the simple overhand knot without untying the main knot, while the ends of the shoelace are held by The Spectator. He covers the simple knot with a handkerchief, and works a moment on the knot, then uncovers it. The knot begins to change, and while The Spectator watches and holds the shoelace ends, The Wizard actually unties the knot!

HOW IT'S DONE:

Here's how you prepare for the trick. Take a new, unused shoelace about 18 inches long. Tie a simple "overhand" knot in it as shown here. An overhand knot is the simplest knot, just one end passed over the other and under it again. Keep it loose. Tie the ends together, using as complicated a knot as you can tie. Try doing double and triple loops, so that the knot is a lump, rather than a long, repeated series of simple knots. Allow about two inches of shoelace to stick out at each end.

You should be seated at a table, with The Spectator seated opposite you. Give The Spectator the ends of the loop to hold. Tell him not to let go. Now place a table napkin or a handkerchief over the simple knot, and put both your hands under the covering. (See illustration B.) Work at it a bit, saying how complicated this task is. Enlarge the loop of the knot as you speak. From time to time, lift up the cover on your side to look at the knot while frowning and shaking your head. At one point, you will shift the cover so it conceals the big knot. Here's where you do the trick. (See illustration C.) You take the lace at the two points shown here, and pull your hands apart, slowly but firmly. Allow the handkerchief to cover the end of the big knot momentarily, as you shift it about. Then pull tight. The simple overhand knot will blend in with the rest of the complicated knot, and the simple knot has vanished!

There is still a problem. The Spectator did not see the simple knot go away, and he may suspect what you've done. So, you move your hands back to the center of the shoelace, and tie a false knot into it. Illustration D will show how. Make a small loop, bring up a folded bit of the lace, push it through the loop, and tighten the loop. Arrange this false knot so that the folded bit does not show. Pull the shoelace tight until the folded part enters the "knot" you've just formed, then take the handkerchief or napkin away.

Now The Spectator sees what he believes is the original knot, still tied. When you tug at each side of this "knot," it pops out of existence!

Here's a variation that you can try when you are more accustomed to the trick: instead of forming the false knot as described above, you can just loop the lace as shown (see illustration E), keeping your finger and thumb over the point shown by the arrow. This will look like the original loose overhand knot, but of course there is no real knot there. Putting your fingers into the loops of this false knot, and rubbing the lace between your hands, you can make it look like the knot slowly vanishes.

Here's the good part. To do this trick for the next Spectator, all you have to do is undo the original genuine knot, which emerges like new from the complicated knot!

One more thing. This trick was actually used by a "spirit medium" many years ago to convince a prominent scientist that the spiritualist had supernatural powers. So don't ever underestimate these simple tricks. They can fool anybody if they are done properly!

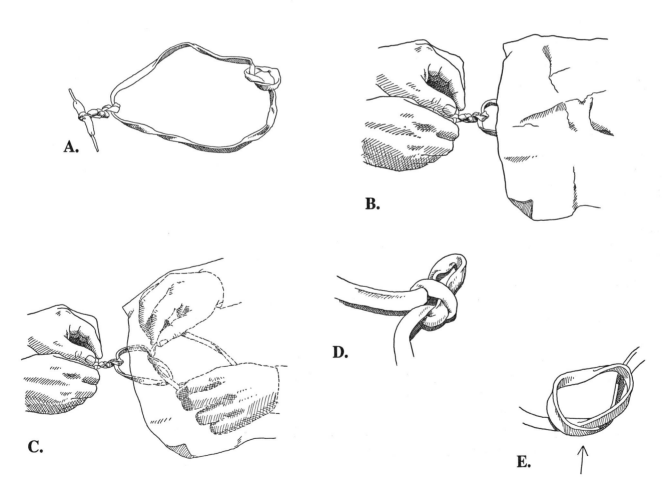

A.

B.

C.

D.

E.

MASSIMO POLIDORO
Italy

Massimo is a young magi who has distinguished himself in Italy, where there is an active magic organization. He also works with the *Comitato Italiano per il Controllo delle Affermazioni sul Paranormale* (The Italian Committee for Control of Claims of the Paranormal), which investigates psychic claims. There is no aspect of the art that does not interest Massimo, and he has put in long hours manipulating playing cards and studying mental tricks to perfect his performance.

Massimo first began learning English about the time he became interested in the Beatles, the legendary musical group. He studied their rise to the top of the entertainment world, and turned out a newsletter called "HELP!" which he wrote, printed and distributed to Beatles fans all around his country. He also picked up an education as an accountant, a job he could do if his aspirations for a magical career didn't work out. He speaks several languages and has considerable musical skills as well.

This trick, which Massimo learned when he was very young, is described in one of the earliest books on magic ever written. It was a good trick then, hundreds of years ago, and it is still a good trick. It follows Oleg Medvedev's contribution because it is a similar trick that is done with ordinary string, rather than a shoelace. You can give away the string when the trick is completed.

RESTORED STRING
THE EFFECT:

The Wizard shows The Spectator a loop of firmly tied string. He takes scissors and cuts a piece right out of the loop on the side opposite the knot. He then wraps the string around his hand, and offers the end to The Spectator to hold. As The Spectator unwinds the string from The Wizard's hand, he sees that it is one piece again, and the knot has disappeared, too! The string may be kept by The Spectator as a souvenir.

This illusion proves that some old tricks never get stale! It's as fresh today as when it was first described in an early book on magic tricks. "Hocus-Pocus Junior," printed in 1763, was more popularly known because of its association with Harry Kellar, a famous American magician who performed many years ago.

HOW IT'S DONE:

You will use two pieces of ordinary, soft white string. One piece should be about 24 inches long and the other about three inches long. Tie the short piece around the middle of the longer piece, tying a regular double knot. (See illustration A.)

Next, you must glue together the loose ends of the long string. Do this by cutting both ends on an angle, using sharp scissors. (See illustration B.) Moisten the cut ends with a little white glue, and roll the wet ends together so the string appears continuous. Make sure your hands are very clean, or you'll have a grey joining point!

Now you have everything ready. The string loop has a fake joining knot in its center, and the glued-together point is opposite that center. Show The Spectator your string loop. Holding it at the points shown in illustration A, tug sharply to "prove" that the knot is secure. Now cut the string twice, with scissors, on each side of the glued section. (See illustration C.) This cuts out the entire glued part, which you throw aside.

Hold one end of the string in your left hand and begin wrapping the other end of the string around your fingers. (See illustration D.) As the fake knot comes into your right hand, just continue wrapping, and allow the knot to slide along and off the end of the string. (See illustration E.) You can get rid of this small end simply by putting it in your pocket while The Spectator is busy with the next part of the trick.

Ask The Spectator to take hold of the loose end of the string. Slowly unwind it from your hand, and leave it hanging in his hand. The Spectator can see that the string is in one piece!

For an even greater effect, substitute a real piece of unglued string for the piece you cut out, and leave that behind for The Spectator to puzzle over!

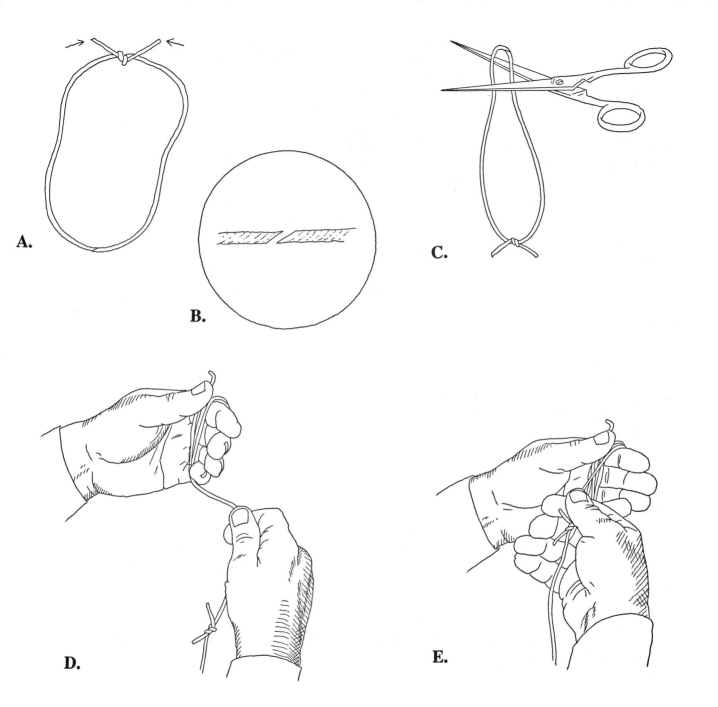

A.

B.

C.

D.

E.

DEAN GUNNARSON
Canada

The cold winters in Winnipeg, Canada don't bother Dean Gunnarson much because he is usually off with brother Todd touring in a van loaded with his unusual equipment. He carries handcuffs, lockpicks, antique padlocks, miles of rope and chain, and a collection of straitjackets, prison locks, manacles and cages. His business requires constant study and invention. He's an escape artist, and in my opinion the best in his profession.

Not many people pursue this branch of the magical art. It requires strength, cunning and great mechanical skill to take on all the obstacles of the challenging act that Dean has perfected. He is the first one to tell newcomers, "Don't take chances. *Know* what you're doing before you start, or you'll get into big trouble!" Those are very wise words.

Dean Gunnarson is closely connected with the Society of Young Magicians (SYM), an affiliate of the Society of American Magicians. The SYM welcomes younger folks who are interested in learning about magic, and Dean tells me that more and more young women are joining the SYM — another welcome sign that old barriers are dropping away. Magic is a hobby and/or a profession that welcomes all comers, and if *you* are interested, contact your local SYM. You'll find contact information in the back of this book.

Dean trained in the fundamentals of magic before he specialized in escape artistry. Here is his contribution. I know that you'll find this trick very entertaining!

THE HOUDINI COIN
THE EFFECT:

The Wizard and The Spectator are seated at a table. The Wizard asks The Spectator to mark a coin with a pen by writing the initial "H" on it, standing for the name, "Houdini." That's so he can identify it later. The Wizard then takes a piece of paper about four inches square and folds the coin into it, forming a small square package. He raps it on the table or on a glass to prove the coin is still in the paper. He places a book on top of the packet, and asks The Spectator to place his hand on the book for security. The Wizard makes a strange face, puts his hand over his mouth, coughs, and the marked coin drops onto the table. When the book is lifted, the paper packet is then torn into tiny pieces to show that the packet is empty.

HOW IT'S DONE:

These trick is all in the way you fold the paper. Follow the illustrations. First, have the coin marked with a felt-tip pen. You should use a quarter for best results. Place the coin just below the center on the square of paper (not printed paper), as shown in illustration A. The Spectator should be sitting across from you.

Fold the paper edge nearest to you, up and away from yourself, so it covers the coin, overlapping it by about a quarter of an inch. (See illustration B.) Now pick up the coin-plus-paper and hold it so The Spectator is now looking at what was the bottom side before you picked it up. Fold each side away from you, allowing a quarter inch on either side, so there is some space around the coin inside the paper. (See illustration C.) Make sharp folds. Then fold the top edge *away* from you, making a sharp fold along the single edge of paper. (See illustration D.)

Reach your right thumb up and over the top of the packet, grasping it between the thumb and first finger. It will be held as shown in illustration E. Rap the packet on a glass or hard table top to prove the coin is still there. Press your thumb down around the edge of the coin to make an impression of the coin in the paper.

Now you make the important move. Tipping up the packet, allow the coin to slide out of the opening in the top and into your hand. (See illustration F.) Grasp the coin in your palm, then place the packet on the table, making sure it does not pop up, since the coin isn't there to weigh it down. Place a book or other object on top of it, and remark to The Spectator that the Houdini coin is now securely imprisoned.

Pause, then bring your hand to your mouth and cover it, as shown in illustration G. With a slight cough, allow the coin to drop "from your mouth" (actually from your hand) onto the table.

Houdini has escaped again!

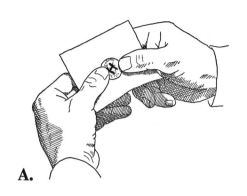

A.

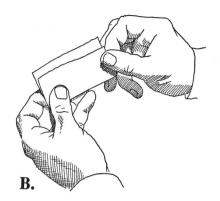

B.

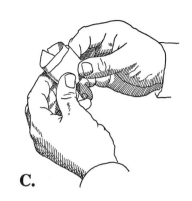

C.

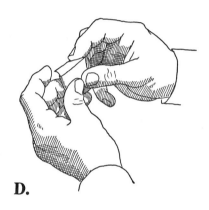

D.

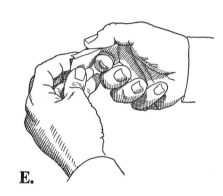

E.

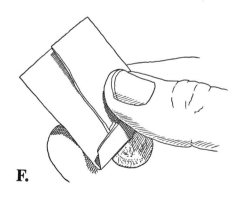

F.

G.

49

HARRY BLACKSTONE
U.S.A.

Ask anyone to start naming famous magicians, and the name Blackstone comes up right away. One of the biggest, best and most exciting magic shows that ever filled a stage with wonders and thrilled an audience to the limit belonged to a charming fuzzy-haired Wizard named Harry Blackstone. I first saw Harry when I was just twelve years old. That experience determined the course of the rest of my life. He was so friendly, so encouraging and so kind to me when I was a child, that I just knew I had to try to be what he was — a magician.

Today, old Harry would be more than proud to see what his son, Harry Jr., has done to elevate the art of magic. With the same elegant, commanding presence and ready wit, the second generation of the magical Blackstone family has met every expectation of the theater world and has more than fulfilled the hopes of his peers. An evening with the Blackstone Show is an evening no one will ever forget.

Whether he is causing an elephant to vanish, changing Gaye, his lovely wife and assistant, into a 300-pound Bengal tiger, or charming his Spectators with the beautiful Floating Light Bulb, Harry Blackstone earns his reputation as a Wizard of the highest order. He makes a theater come alive with wonders.

This is one of the tricks that Mr. Blackstone might choose to show you if you were to visit him backstage some night. He considers this an impromptu miracle that you can do at a moment's notice.

THE AMAZING BLACK HOLE
THE EFFECT:

At the request of The Wizard, The Spectator shuffles a pack of cards, and places it face up on the back of this magic book. The Wizard takes a business card and inserts it half way down the pack then lifts the upper part of the pack to give The Spectator a peek at the card located at that position. The Wizard asks The Spectator to pick up the pack and find the card he just peeked at, while watching the magic book carefully all the while. The Spectator finds that the card he has just seen is no longer in the pack. When he lifts the back cover of the magic book, however, he finds the selected card there, face up, as if it had penetrated the book cover. It is resting on a pattern on the last page of the book, with the heading above it: HOW DID I GET HERE? ONLY (The Wizard) KNOWS!

HOW IT'S DONE:

This is a trick for which you will have to prepare a special prop. It's rather easy to do. You may have to spoil a deck of cards, but, as you'll see, it's really worth it. You need a full deck of cards and an extra playing card as well. If you're lucky, you can probably get a single spare playing card from your local magic shop. Magic shop proprietors are generally very nice folks. Just show them this book, and they'll probably help you out.

Say you have an extra king of hearts. Obtain a regular business card, and some "frosty" Scotch tape. That's the kind that's invisible when you press it down tightly on a piece of paper — not the shiny kind.

Look at illustration A to see how you cut the playing card. The piece of playing card you will use must be just a bit smaller (about an eighth of an inch) from top to bottom than the business card. Cut it off perfectly square, and line up the two cards at the bottom. Wrap a piece of Scotch tape from the back of the playing card around to the front of the business card, thus making a sort of hinge with the tape. Press the tape down firmly. This is your gimmick card, which looks like a perfectly ordinary business card when seen from the front.

From your regular deck of cards, remove the king of hearts and place it, face down, in the rectangle you'll find on the last page of this book. However, you must first enter your name in the space after the word "ONLY" below the rectangle.

Close this book. It becomes one of your props. Place the book, face down, on the table. Put the gimmick card in your shirt pocket so that when you reach in and take it out, it will look to The Spectator like a regular business card. Of course, you keep the hinged half of the playing card held tightly against the back and out of sight.

Now you're ready to do the trick. Offer the deck to The Spectator for shuffling. Have him place the deck face up on the back cover of the book, in the rectangle you'll find on the rear cover. Remove the gimmick card from your pocket, holding the hinged piece of playing card tightly against the back, so it doesn't show. Ask The Spectator, "How far down shall I go? Half-way, three-quarters, or where?" He tells you, and you insert the gimmick card into the deck, sliding it to a position where the piece of the king of hearts will line up with the other cards. (See illustration B.)

Now, lift the upper section of the deck, along with the business card. This leaves the piece of the king of hearts facing The Spectator, as in illustration C. Ask The Spectator to remember that card. Now allow the deck to close up again, and withdraw the gimmick card. Casually put it away in your inside pocket. Of course, the attached piece of the king of hearts goes with it.

Next, instruct The Spectator to pick up the deck and look through it for the card he peeked at. You should also mention that you have not touched nor tried to open the magic book. The Spectator will not find his card, so you ask him to look inside the back cover. The face down card in the book is his card. The message written above it says it all.

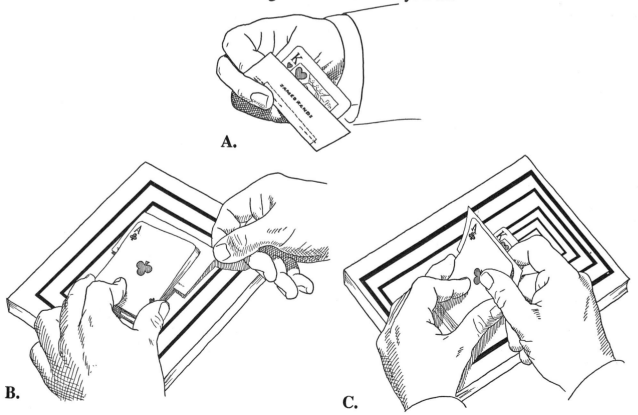

A.

B.

C.

BILLY McCOMB
Ireland

Visitors to the Magic Castle in Hollywood, California, can't fail to notice Billy McComb, for he struts about this private club looking every inch The Wizard. He came to us from England many years ago, and he is a familiar figure at the Castle when he is not working aboard luxury cruise ships around the world.

Billy was born in Belfast, Ireland. With his crafty smile, he likes to say that his mother tells everyone that the year he was born was not a good year for *anything*! He moved to England and came under the influence of such magicians as Dante, Goldin, and Levante, who taught him much about the magical art. He has worked many times at Buckingham Palace entertaining the Royal Family.

Billy has been a good friend to me for many decades. I first met him when we were working in a theater in London, and he was the Master of Ceremonies. He has so many credits to his name, including many books on magic, that it would be difficult to list even a portion of them. He is one of the grand masters of our art.

Billy McComb does everything with a distinctive twist; his rapid-fire jokes are an essential part of his unique stage show. In sharing the following trick with you, he asks that you put *your* twist on it, rather than imitating his style of performance.

SORTING OUT THE CARDS
THE EFFECT:

The Wizard deals off a small packet of eleven cards from a deck. He then proceeds to deal the first card into The Spectator's hand, and places the next card underneath the packet. The Wizard repeats this process until all the cards are dealt. Picking up the packet, he turns it over and shows that the eleven cards are now in order from Ace to Jack. As he repeats the process several times, more strange combinations come to light. The cards are next arranged with all the odd cards together, and all the even cards together. Then they come alternating hearts and spades. This is followed by all the hearts being grouped together, then all the spades. Finally, the packet reorders itself, so that the sequence of ace to Jack has returned.

HOW IT'S DONE:

This is, as Billy admits, more a puzzle than a trick, but it will be very difficult for The Spectator to figure out how to do it. The secret is in the initial arrangement. Reading from the top down, place this sequence of eleven cards on the top of the deck: six of spades, ten of clubs, five of clubs, eight of spades, four of clubs, jack of diamonds, three of diamonds, seven of hearts, two of hearts, nine of diamonds, ace of hearts. The other cards can be in any order.

Pick up the deck and deal off the top eleven cards, one at a time, into The Spectator's open hand. This reverses the original order. Put the remainder of the deck aside. Picking up the packet, you now deal off the first card, face up, into The Spectator's hand. Place the next card, face down, at the bottom of the packet. Again, deal the next card face up into The Spectator's hand and deal the next one to the bottom. Repeat this until all cards are gone. You'll see that the cards will be dealt out in order, ace to Jack! Pick up the packet, turn it over, and repeat the dealing procedure. This time, the next sequence — all odds together and then all evens together — will show up, and so on until the cards return to their original order. The third time, the cards will alternate, red, black, red, black, etc. The fourth time, all reds will be dealt down first, followed by all the blacks! The fifth time, they'll return to the original order, Ace to Jack.

Of course, you will provide running commentary to go along with all of this. For example, the first deal you can simply read out the numbers as they are dealt into The Spectator's hand, "ace, 2, 3, 4, 5, 6, 7, 8, 9 and jack." Then you say, as you perform the second deal, "And here are the odd cards [as you deal them] ace, 3, 5, 7, 9 and the jack, followed by the even cards, 4, 8, 2, 10, and 6." The third deal you say, "But now let's alternate reds and blacks. Red, black, red, black..." to the end. The fourth time, you can say, "But here are all the red cards, [and you count out the first six cards] red, red, red, red, red, and red, followed by [and you deal out the remaining five cards] black, black, black, black and black."

Until you've done this little demonstration for someone, you won't realize how crazy they can go, trying to do the same thing! To *really* drive them nuts, try doing a false shuffle (though this will take some practice) with the deck after the eleven cards are correctly placed on top, and you're ready to perform. Just shuffle in a regular fashion, but don't disturb the top eleven cards. The Spectator will think that just any group of cards was dealt out in this strange fashion, and he may attribute alien powers to you!

ROBERT STEINER
U.S.A.

I'd like you to meet a valued friend of mine. I've known him all my life, and we have worked together on many projects. Robert Steiner is one of those folks who makes his magic on a "semi-professional" basis. He works during the week as a chartered accountant, but at nights and on weekends, he becomes a medieval-style Wizard, often dressed in his interesting Merlin costume. He can be spotted easily at fairs and other such outdoor functions by his peaked hat.

Bob is the National President of The Society of American Magicians (S.A.M.). He invites you to inquire about becoming a member of the S.A.M. and share in the fun and learning that take place wherever the organization has a local branch. The address is in the back of this book.

Magician Steiner started in magic when he was a young boy, and now he uses his performances to educate children against the abuse of drugs. He also gives presentations to police and medical groups on fraud and mistaken beliefs. Look for Bob's book, *Don't Get Taken*. It deals with scams and swindles.

He wants to share this excellent prediction trick with you. It's a real winner!

A SURE PREDICTION

THE EFFECT:

The Wizard casually places three piles of playing cards on the table. He writes out a prediction on a scrap of paper, and places it in The Spectator's pocket. The Spectator is now asked to point to *any* of the three piles, but is also told that he must try to avoid the pile that The Wizard has already named in his written prediction. No matter what pile is chosen, The Wizard is *always* right!

HOW IT'S DONE:

Arrange your deck of cards so that the first twelve cards, in order from the top, are: six of hearts, four of clubs, queen of clubs, three of hearts, three of spades, three of clubs, three of diamonds, king of spades, nine of clubs, two of hearts, eight of hearts, and ace of diamonds. The rest can be in any order at all. In fact, I've specified the first three cards and the last five cards only to make the piles appear random.

In placing your three piles of cards, toss down the first three cards in the first pile, the next four cards in the second pile, and the last five in the third pile. Don't let it appear that you're counting the cards as you lay them down. Square the piles up casually, write out your prediction, and sign it. It will read:

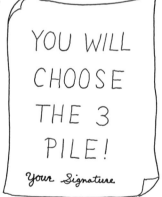

YOU WILL
CHOOSE
THE 3
PILE!
Your Signature

Fold the paper up and have The Spectator place it, unread, in his pocket.

The Spectator only has three choices. But tease him. Tell him that you have predicted which pile he is going to choose, and that he cannot avoid doing so, no matter how hard he tries. Tell him that if he changes his mind, he can do so only once. Then ask him to choose. After he has indicated his choice, ask him, "Now you have ten seconds to change your mind. Decide!" And you begin counting off the seconds. When you reach a count of ten, tell The Spectator, "You have made your decision. And it is just as I predicted!"

Now what do you do? Well, it all depends on The Spectator's decision. If he chooses the first pile, you simply spread out each of the little piles, leaving them face down. You say, "These piles are different. This one (you indicate the second pile) has four cards in it. This one (you point to the third pile) has five cards in it. But *this* one (you indicate the pile he chose) has exactly *three* cards in it. It is the three pile. Please look at my prediction." As he unfolds it, take it from him, and read, "You will take the *three* pile!" And, of course, you are right.

If The Spectator chooses the second pile, pick up the first pile, face down, and add it to the third pile. Turn all of these eight cards over and spread them out. You say to The Spectator, "As you can see, these are all random cards. But the pile that *you* chose (you turn over the cards of that pile, fanning them out, face up) contains all *threes*. This pile is the three pile. Please read the prediction I wrote." And you proceed as above, reading it for him.

If The Spectator chooses the third pile, you say to him, "You had a perfectly free choice of the cards you wanted. There were one, two, three of them. [As you say that, you touch each with your finger.] You chose the third pile. Please unfold the prediction I wrote out." Again, you read the prediction for him, but this time, you read it, "You will take the *third* pile!" And at this point, you sweep all the cards together, dropping them back atop the deck.

Don't perform this trick for the same Spectator twice!

MICHAEL CHEN
Jamaica

When you have a natural feature, it's always smart to use it. Michael Chen lives on the small island of Jamaica, where every variety of ethnic origin can be found. He discovered when he was young and interested in doing magic, that magicians often try to appear Oriental when they perform. Michael took advantage of the happy fact that he already looks, walks, talks and performs in an Oriental fashion. Soon, he began learning tricks that used rice, porcelain bowls, colored paper, chopsticks and other artifacts of Chinese life. The result has been a successful magic career.

Today, magician Chen can be seen in the night clubs of Jamaica and the United States, levitating a pretty assistant on the point of a huge silver scimitar or performing the famous Rice Bowl Trick — one of the most famous and elegant routines in magical history. Always looking for new and interesting ideas, he travels extensively, working as both a magician and a photographer, and is able to visit with magicians in many distant countries. It's fortunate that Michael doesn't have to choose between magic and photography, for he excels at both arts.

Michael Chen describes, just for you, a great "pocket" trick that you can carry with you just about anywhere! I recommend this trick highly because it is so easy and very effective.

THE BUDDHA PAPERS

THE EFFECT:

The Wizard shows The Spectator a square, folded packet of paper, which is placed flat on the table. Unfolded, the packet holds a smaller, similar folded packet, and — you guessed it — there's a third, even smaller folded paper inside *that* one. All three papers are laid out on top of one another. A borrowed, marked dime is placed inside the smallest packet, and all three papers are carefully re-folded to form the original square packet. The Spectator is asked merely to blow on the packet. The packet is once again unfolded. But this time, when the innermost paper is opened, The Spectator's dime has changed into a penny! The whole process is repeated: finally the dime is recovered for The Spectator, and his money is returned to him.

HOW IT'S DONE:

It's pretty simple; first, you must make up a small prop for yourself, the packet of paper. It can be made in different sizes, but for now I suggest that these measurements are best:

Outside square: 6" x 6"
Next square: 5" x 5"
Inner square: 3" x 3"

You will need *two* sets of these three papers. Use very thin paper, but the paper cannot be transparent. "Newsprint" paper is ideal. You should use three different colors of paper, as Michael does when doing this trick.

Place both outside paper squares together and fold them as if they were one piece. This ensures that they will both look the same. Fold the papers over one-third of the way, as shown in illustration A, then one-third the other way, until you have two small packets. Put these aside and do the same with the next smaller squares, and finally with the smallest. Make all your creases sharp and clean.

Assemble them this way: Nest a set of three packets, each smaller one inside the other. Repeat with the second set. (See illustration B.) Now attach the two sets by gluing the back of one large square to the back of the other. (See illustration C.) This is your prop!

To prepare your prop, open one set of squares and place a penny in the innermost packet, as in illustration B. Then re-fold the packet. Make a tiny pencil mark on the *other* side of the prop, so you will recognize that side. Now you are ready to perform.

Take the prop from your pocket and place it down on the table so that the pencil-marked side is uppermost. You will have to hold the prop down, since it tends to pop up because of the duplicate set of packets. Open the outer square, holding the packet flat on the table. Open each of the other two squares in the same way. Borrow a dime from The Spectator, promising to return it. Place the dime in the inner paper, and re-fold the set of squares.

Pick up the prop, holding it as in illustration D, and turn it over as you hold it up to The Spectator's mouth, asking that he blow on it "for good luck." You can easily turn the packet over, unnoticed by The Spectator, if you handle it just this way. (See illustration E.) The Spectator doesn't know about the duplicate set of papers on the other side, and now when you lay the prop flat on the table, he thinks you are merely re-opening the same papers. When you get to the inner paper he finds that his dime has changed into a penny.

You now reverse and repeat the whole process in order to recover The Spectator's dime — unless you want to make a 9-cent profit. I don't think that's worth the fist-fight that may result.

Variations on the above: Place a tiny note in with the penny, reading, "IOU 9¢." If you think that's too dangerous, try this: Prepare a third single set of papers that you can leave around so The Spectator can satisfy his curiosity. Inside the inner folded paper, put a small card with the printed message, "My, my! You're *so* curious!" Or, make your prop from colored comics, using two identical pages from the same issue. In this way, each set of papers will look *exactly* the same, and The Spectator will never suspect a switch!

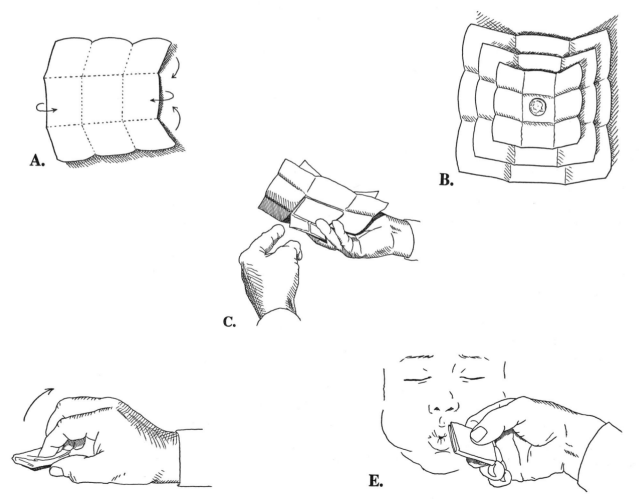

A.

B.

C.

D

E.

HARRY MAURER
U.S.A.

Most magicians are lucky enough to come under the influence of a professional who helps them get started. In Harry Maurer's case, it was his grandfather who pulled coins out of his ears, thus inspiring another potential magician. As a teen, Harry worked with a group of talented young performers known as the "Show Biz Kids," who entertained in New Jersey. He then began working independently, first in restaurants — for six hours a day — and then in night clubs. He even got special permission to be away from school for certain engagements.

After studying theater at The School of Creative and Performing Arts at Rutgers University, magician Maurer took on the night club circuit in earnest. Along the way, he almost became a comedian, rather than a magician. But magic won out. He is now a prominent Atlantic City Casino entertainer, and was even voted as "Atlantic City's Entertainer of the Year — Best Opening Act."

Harry's advice for young performers: "It is much better to perform a few tricks well than twenty tricks badly. Spend as much time learning how to make your magic fun and interesting as you do actually learning how to do the tricks. Most of all, have fun doing them!"

THE NEXT CARD I TURN OVER
THE EFFECT:

A deck of cards is shuffled by The Spectator, then placed on the front cover of this magic book, face down. The Wizard cuts the pack where The Spectator directs him to and The Spectator looks at and remembers the card at that place. Then The Wizard replaces the cut. The Spectator then picks up the deck, cuts it several more times, and hands it to The Wizard. The Wizard begins dealing cards from the top of the pack, one at a time, onto the table, turning each one over as he places it down. After a while, he peeks at the next card on the deck and asks The Spectator, "Will you bet me that the next card I turn over won't be your card?" The Spectator eagerly agrees to the bet, since he has seen his selected card already dealt down on the table! When he accepts the bet, The Wizard merely reaches into the pile of already-dealt cards and turns over the correct card, thus winning the bet!

HOW IT'S DONE:

You'll use a regular, well shuffled deck of cards. You'll also use this magic book as a prop. The front cover has a highly reflective "dragon" hologram, which will enable you to perform this miracle. It's just like a little mirror.

Tell The Spectator that this magic book has a special "E.S.P. detector" built into it that will enable you to read his mind. Offer to demonstrate. Hand him the deck of cards, and instruct him to shuffle it. Now, you tell him to place the deck on the front cover of the book, face down. You ask him how far down he would like you to cut the deck. Whatever his answer, you cut off approximately that number of cards from the deck. As you lift off the packet of cards, bring it over the shiny surface of the book cover, while pointing with your left hand at the other part of the deck. (See illustration A.) You can look into the shiny surface and see a clear reflection of the bottom card in the packet you are holding. Memorize that card. This is what we call the "key" card.

You now ask The Spectator to look at the top card, at the place where the deck was cut. He does so, making sure that you don't see it. The Spectator leaves his card on top of the pile. Now you replace the cut-off packet back on top of the other cards, and ask The Spectator to pick up the deck and cut it three times, while he is thinking of his chosen card — the one he looked at.

No matter how many times The Spectator cuts the deck, his chosen card and your key card will remain in the same relationship. The *only* separation of those two cards that can occur would be if The Spectator happens to cut the deck exactly between them, and that is a separate miracle we'll deal with in a moment.

You pick up the deck now, and begin dealing cards, one at a time, from the top, turning each one over as you toss it down on the table. You instruct The Spectator, "Please, don't tell me if you see your card. I'll trust the E.S.P. detector to tell me where it is."

Eventually, you will run into your "key" card, and you know that the *next* card is The Spectator's chosen card. Don't react to this, but remember what the chosen card is. Of course, you can now forget the key card, because it only served to identify the chosen card for you! Just keep right on dealing, about four or five cards more (see illustration B); then stop, slyly peek underneath at the next card you are about to deal, and ask The Spectator, "Will you bet me that the next card I turn over *won't* be your card?"

Of course, The Spectator will be very sure that the "next" card isn't his, since he has already seen it as you dealt it onto the table. As soon as he agrees to bet with you, you reach down to the table and you *turn his card over!* Remember, you said, "the next card I *turn over*," not, "the next card I *deal onto the table*!"

What about the special case, mentioned above, in which The Spectator has cut between the two cards? To allow for this, always glance at the bottom card of the deck after you pick it up. If, and only if, that is the "key" card, you will change your treatment of the trick. You will merely tell The Spectator that you are going to make his chosen card rise to the top of the deck. Then, without doing *anything*, you simply announce the miracle, because that's where his chosen card will be!

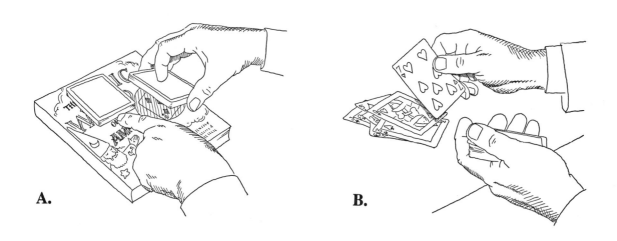

A.   **B.**

MARTIN COTTET
Switzerland

At a convention of magicians (yes, we have conventions, just like shoe salesmen and politicians!) in Madrid, Spain, a few years ago, I met two exciting young artists who worked together as The United Artists. Martin Cottet and Marco Tempest performed intricate manipulations, sharing the objects they handled so that their audience could not tell who performed what bit of sleight-of-hand! I brought them to the United States, where they won all sorts of performing prizes and honors.

While Marco continues to perform in Europe and the Far East, Martin is in the United States again, working a "single" act. Since his first experience in show business was as a dancer, he believes that body movement should be a very important part of his act, and he uses dancing to improve the effect of his illusions. He says, "I created an act with Marco Tempest in which we performed with one person standing directly behind the other. In this way we packed in a lot of moves using four arms but only one body. As a solo artist I have more freedom. I combine classical dance with electric boogie to present my concept of dance with magic."

Martin gives much credit for his success to magicians like Rocco, Vito Lupo, and Otto Wesseley, who have inspired him and helped him to learn and develop his ideas. He also gives much credit to his Christian outlook, which has convinced him that "positive thinking can make all things possible."

Besides magic, Martin Cottet is an accomplished airbrush artist and musician who sings with his group, Flavor Blue. This trick that he offers you involves many more colors than just blue.

COLOR TELEPATHY
THE EFFECT:

The Wizard empties the contents of a box of crayons onto a table. (Crayons may even be supplied by The Spectator.) He selects eight or nine of them for the test, and hands them to The Spectator, who is seated across from him. The Spectator places them all under the table, selects one, and without looking at it, hands it to The Wizard under the table. Feeling it, The Wizard announces the color of the unseen crayon, even though The Spectator doesn't know it! The Spectator then produces it as proof. This is repeated several times successfully.

HOW IT'S DONE:

You need only a small piece of white cardboard, about 1 inch square, for a prop.

You and The Spectator are seated across from one another at a table. You bring out the crayon box, and empty it, choosing a few crayons for the test. You must choose vivid, easily-identifiable colors. Yellow and white are not recommended, for reasons you'll soon discover. Hand the selected crayons to The Spectator and ask him to place them below the table, mix them in his hands, and then select one for a test.

As soon as he has selected one, ask to feel it below the table. Place both hands under the table, take hold of the crayon, and brush the white card against it, making a colored mark on the white card. Be sure that The Spectator does not let go of the crayon as you feel it. Continue feeling the crayon with your right hand, and bring your left hand — with the card — into your lap. A quick glance downward will tell you what the selected color is!

You can repeat this just about as often as you wish.

NATHAN BURTON
U.S.A.

Magicians often choose to adopt a specialty. Some are escape artists, others work with birds, and many do close-up table work. Nathan Burton, who is known as Burtoni, works exclusively with water and fish! He produces gallons of water from nowhere, catches fish on a magical fishing-rod, and fills an aquarium with dozens of live goldfish. As if that weren't enough, the audience sees a huge trout appear from his bare hands. At the end of his act, Nathan leaves a very wet stage and enough fish to supply a pet shop!

With this novel approach, Burtoni seems destined to make quite a "splash" in the world of magic. Since water-and-fish tricks are really only for professionals, Nathan has chosen to teach you one of the tricks he used before he adopted his specialty. It's easily learned, and can be a very pretty illusion.

THE HOLY HANDKERCHIEF
THE EFFECT:

The Wizard takes a quarter from The Spectator and covers it with a handkerchief, twisting the quarter into the center of the cloth. Thus imprisoned, the quarter seems secure. But with a little coaxing from The Wizard, the coin slowly penetrates the cloth and drops into The Spectator's hand!

HOW IT'S DONE:

You will need an ordinary handkerchief or a light weight table napkin, plus a borrowed coin. Ask The Spectator to mark the coin (a "Sharpie" marker is ideal for this). Hold the coin between your right thumb and first finger, with the thumb on top. (See illustration A.) Lay the opened handkerchief on your left hand, and throw it over the right hand so that the coin is now in the center, covered by the handkerchief.

Now, from the top, push the first finger of your left hand in between your right thumb and the coin, (see illustration B) thus pinching a good fold of the handkerchief between the thumb and coin. Next, reach with your left hand to the edge of the handkerchief nearest The Spectator and raise that edge back towards your right wrist, exposing the coin. (See illustration C.) Say to The Spectator, "Take a good look at your money. It may be the last time you see it!"

Now you do the tricky move. Simply flip the entire handkerchief forward toward The Spectator, covering the coin, but holding the handkerchief firmly between your right thumb and the coin, where you gathered a fold before. (See illustration D.) It *appears* as if you have simply covered the coin again, when actually it is *outside* and underneath the handkerchief, not seen by The Spectator.

Move your right thumb a bit so as to draw a good inch or so of the cloth over the coin, to make sure it's covered from sight. With your left hand, begin twisting the part of the handkerchief that is a few inches away from the coin so that the coin appears to be securely imprisoned inside. (See illustration E.) Instruct The Spectator to hold on to the handkerchief where it's twisted up.

Now begin working away at the place where the coin is held, as if trying to make it penetrate the cloth. Allow the coin to come into view slowly, and the illusion is perfect. (See illustration F.) It seems as if the coin is slipping right through the center of the handkerchief!

As you pull the coin through the handkerchief and hand it over for examination, tell The Spectator, "Careful! It's still hot!" You'd be surprised how many people actually drop the "hot" coin!

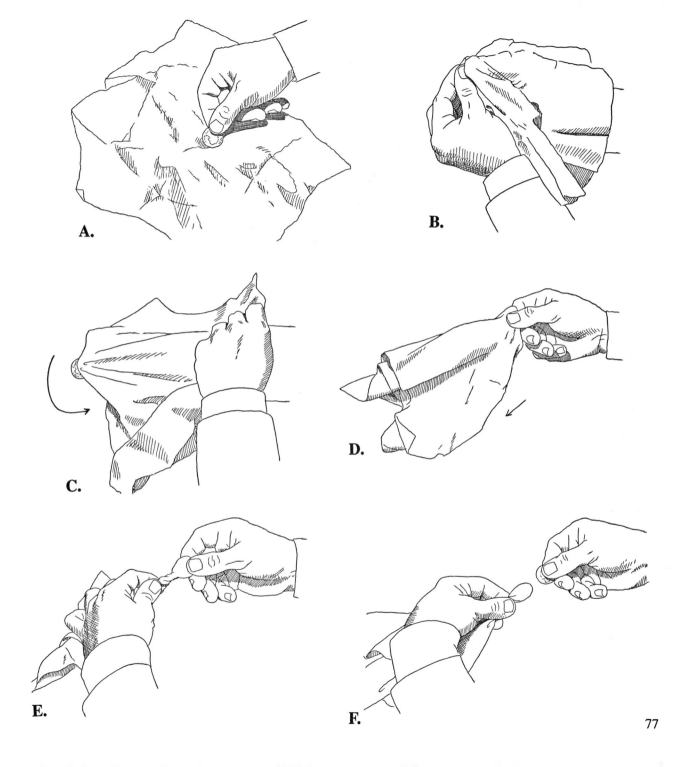

A.

B.

C.

D.

E.

F.

ALEXANDER
Puerto Rico

Not all young magicians want to become professionals. Some, like Alexander, want to be advanced amateurs and enjoy magic as a hobby. Eventually, magic might even be a source of extra income for this talented young man. He also believes that magic will allow him to travel around the world, and I think he's quite right, especially because he speaks both Spanish and English. Ah, but the magic "bug" is very sneaky, and just might bite Alexander when he's not looking. . .

His interest in magic started at a school book sale when he came upon a book outlining simple tricks. Later, he met Federico Navarro, a member of the Society of American Magicians, and began to learn tricks from this master. Not long after, he was invited to do a television show called De Todo Un Poco ("A Little of Everything"). This was only the first of Alexander's many invitations to appear on TV.

Alexander has come under the influence of many famous names in magic, including Gustavo Lorgia, Bill Andrews, Father Cyprian, and Dean Gunnarson. He has learned to perform with ropes, birds, and silk handkerchiefs, and he even does some tricks with fire. His ambition is to make people happy watching his magic, and this contribution will certainly make your Spectator happy.

THE MAGIC HOLE
THE EFFECT:

The Wizard offers his business card, a sharp wooden pencil, and a strong rubber band to The Spectator for examination. The Spectator verifies that these objects are all normal. The Wizard loops the rubber band around the corners of the card. He then punches the pencil through the card so that it passes through the middle of the rubber band. The Spectator is asked to hold both ends of the pencil firmly. Obviously, the pencil cannot move because it is trapped by the rubber band — but as The Wizard removes the rubber band from the card, he snaps it *right through* the firmly-held pencil!

HOW IT'S DONE:

This is an excellent way to hand out business cards, although the cards used for this trick will have holes in them. Whoever carries the cards away will tell everyone about the miracle!

You will need a rubber band that is big enough to be stretched very easily over the business card without bending it, wrapping it diagonally across the corners, as shown in the illustrations.

After showing all the props you are going to use, push the end of the pencil through the center of the card. (See illustration A.) Remove the pencil. Next, loop the rubber band around the card as shown. Now push the pencil back through the hole, and point out to The Spectator that the pencil is definitely surrounded by the rubber band. Held at each end, it cannot escape the rubber band. The Spectator will agree.

Remove the pencil, asking The Spectator to examine it carefully to be sure there are no secret trapdoors in it. As you do this, you will be holding the card in your left hand. as shown. When the rubber band is in place, one side will have long sections of band and the other side will have shorter sections. The side with the longest sections should be facing you.

Here comes the magic move. Ready? As The Spectator is examining the pencil, you will scoop up one of the long sections with your left thumb, and pull it toward the other long section, pushing it across the card past the hole you have already made. (See illustration B.) The Spectator can't see this because he is looking at the other side of the card. (When you are familiar with this trick, you will want to do it with The Spectator looking *down* on the card, and your left thumb *underneath* the card.)

Now push the pencil through the hole in the card *from The Spectator's side,* as in illustration B, and it will not enter the loop of the rubber band. Immediately release the section of rubber band from your thumb, and ask The Spectator to grab each end of the pencil, one end on the side of the card toward him, and the other end on the side away from him.

You are ready for the miracle. With the thumb and first finger of each hand, grab each of the short sections of rubber band that are facing The Spectator. Pull them off and away from the card as in illustration C, keeping the rubber band against the lower side of the pencil. (See illustration D.) Bring the band about an inch closer to yourself and stretch it out, then allow one end to snap loose just by letting it go. While The Spectator held the pencil tightly, the rubber band snapped right through it!

At this point, you give The Spectator your business card and ask him to call you when he needs an excellent magician!

A NOTE: If you have business cards printed up, why not have a 1/2-inch black spot printed in the very center, and label it, "Magic Hole"? Then you can use it for this trick every time!

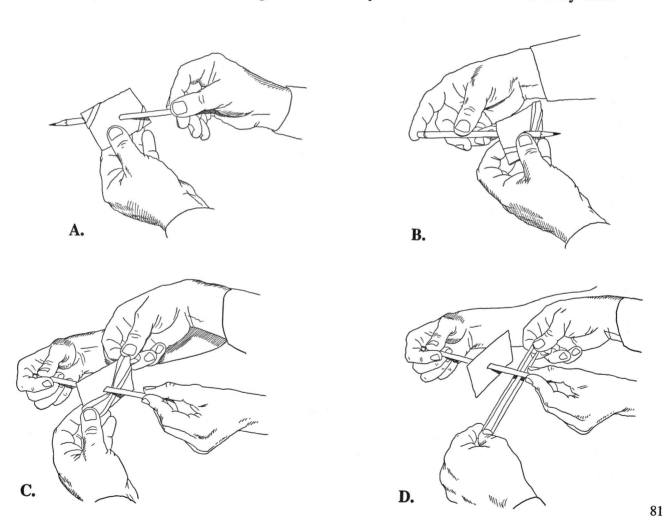

A.

B.

C.

D.

STEVE GOTSON
France

Here is a magician I first met in Spain, at a magician's convention. He is closely connected with the Magicus Journal, a publication printed in France for magicians. Steve's articles on magic have appeared in many magazines for magicians.

In the small province of Drôme in France, Steve Gotson founded a school that teaches magic to eager young students. The kids use such modern tools as videotape to see how well they have performed. Steve certainly likes his chosen work.

Choosing from one of the many tricks that he teaches to his pupils in France, Steve Gotson will share with you a simple yet effective trick that requires only two pencils.

YOU DO AS I DO... IF YOU CAN!

THE EFFECT:

The Wizard shows two ordinary wooden pencils with erasers on the end. He asks The Spectator to imitate several simple moves. He begins by pushing the pencil into and out of his fist several times. The Spectator is able to do this easily, until The Wizard declares that he has now hypnotized The Spectator so that he cannot perform such a simple move. Sure enough, when The Spectator tries, he cannot do it!

HOW IT'S DONE:

Obtain two identical pencils, each having a metal ferrule with an eraser in it. ("Ferrule" is a fancy word for the metal ring that holds the eraser in place.) One pencil will remain as it is. The other — which The Wizard will use — must be specially prepared as follows. Remove the rubber eraser by twisting it out. Wrap a little paper around the ferrule, and using a pair of pliers, twist the ferrule until it comes off. Then replace the eraser into the ferrule.

Sharpen the ordinary pencil, and sharpen *both* ends of the special pencil. Place the extra ferrule over one end of this special pencil.

The sharpening of the pencils must be done with a sharpener that cuts the pencil in a blunt way. Ordinary sharpeners make a long tapered point. You want to use a cheap hand sharpener that produces a *short* cone at the end of the pencil. (See illustration A.)

If you cannot sharpen your pencils this way, there is another solution. Hollow out the inside end of the rubber eraser, so that when you re-insert the sharpened end of the pencil, the graphite tip will not push the eraser out. Perhaps you will be lucky enough to find pencils with extra-long ferrules, in which case this work is not necessary.

Give The Spectator the ordinary pencil; you take the trick one. Stand facing him. Ask him to perform exactly the same moves you do, but inform him that he must do them *as if he were your mirror image.* What you do with your right hand, he will do with his left, as a reflection would.

Start by simply sliding your pencil slowly into one side of your fist and out the other side, point-first (see illustration B) and then eraser-first. He will have no problem following these simple moves. Repeat this, but turn your fist around after the pencil has been slipped into it, and be sure he "reflects" your moves.

After a few of these moves, tell him he is now hypnotized. Wave your hands around and mumble strange words. (I prefer "ugg-ugga-boo, ugga-boo-boo, ugg-ugg." I make no guarantees that this won't make The Spectator break out in a dreadful red rash, so go easy!) Holding the pencil horizontally in your right hand, and concealing the point end in your palm, slowly slide your special pencil, with the fake eraser end first, into your closed left fist. Make *sure* that The Spectator does exactly the same.

As soon as the eraser end is well inside your left hand, grasp the ferrule with your closed fingers and twist the pencil (with your right hand) so the ferrule slides off and is retained inside your left hand. Immediately draw your pencil out of your fist, showing the pointed end, and say, "No, no! I *told* you you'd get it wrong! Do it *this* way!" And you indicate the pointed end going into your fist. Somewhat confused, he will change ends of his pencil.

Now you slowly insert the pointed end into your hand, plugging it back into the ferrule. You watch as The Spectator mirrors your action, then you stop and again scold him. "No, no. Again, you got it wrong. As I told you, you're hypnotized." Now you slowly push the re-assembled pencil through your fist and out the other side. To The Spectator's horror, he sees the *eraser* end come out. You now lift away your right hand, and show your pencil in exactly the opposite position!

A SUGGESTION: Think about having a third, perfectly ordinary pencil in your inner jacket pocket. At the conclusion of this trick, put your prop pencil away, then as it goes into your inner pocket, switch pencils and bring it right back out again, offering to write The Spectator a prescription for his hallucinations!

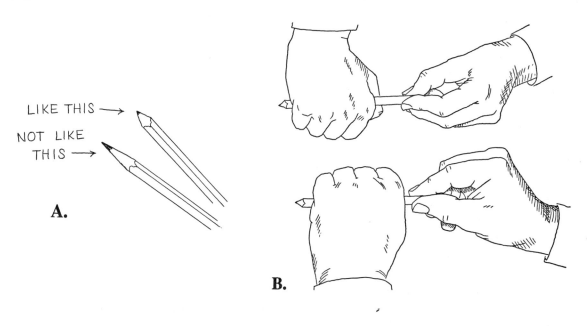

LIKE THIS →

NOT LIKE THIS →

A.

B.

PENN & TELLER
U.S.A.

Stand back! These two are a lot different from most of the magicians who you've met so far in this book. Until you've seen their show — which is always packed to capacity with their adoring fans — you can't really know what Penn (he's the big guy with the red fingernail who does all the talking) and Teller (the smaller one, who doesn't say a word) are all about. Their act is so entertaining, both magically and comically, that the audience is constantly in stitches. The team breaks records everywhere; it played off-Broadway for 22 weeks and on Broadway for 17 more.

These two are hardly limited to the stage. They have made several specials for television, and recently completed *Penn & Teller Get Killed,* a really bizarre film. They appear frequently on the "Late Night with David Letterman" television show, and on "Saturday Night Live."

The magic of Penn & Teller is unique. There's always a twist to it that makes it their own. Their inimitable style shows through in this offering from them. This trick *seems* to go very, very wrong. . . but fortunately, you can count on the team of Penn & Teller to bail you out!

THE TRICK THAT NEVER GOES WRONG
THE EFFECT:

The Wizard, ever confident, shuffles a deck of cards, places it face down on the table, and asks The Spectator to cut the deck and look at the card at that position. The deck is then re-assembled. The Wizard shuffles and cuts several times, appears to have a "psychic vision," then reaches in and produces The Spectator's card. Or so he thinks, because the card turns out to be wrong. The Wizard tries again, but again fails. He misses a third time, and is obviously getting desperate. The Spectator is looking smug.

Suddenly inspired, The Wizard recalls that Penn & Teller have a solution to such a problem. He turns to the back of this book, and looks for the "EMERGENCY SECTION wherein Penn & Teller save your wretched skin when a trick goes wrong."

The Wizard performs a weird, phony-scientific ritual and finally reveals the name of the selected card actually printed right in the book!

HOW IT'S DONE:

This involves what magicians call a "force." You start with the force card (for this trick you must use the three of clubs) on the top of the deck. You can shuffle this deck as much as you want, as long as you don't disturb that top card. Practice doing this, using any shuffle, but retaining the top card in its place.

Tell The Spectator that you believe in E.S.P. (Penn & Teller want to be sure I tell you that this is a big fat lie. They say that no one with any brains believes in such stuff. As this pair of magicians like to point out, in magic nobody thinks you're a crook no matter how much you lie!) Now comes the subtle part. Ask The Spectator to cut off a portion of the deck and set it down about a foot away from the remainder of the deck, squared up. He does this. (See illustration A.) Now instruct him to pick up the remainder of the deck and place it *across* the cut-off portion (see illustration B), saying as you do this, "Just put it here, cross-wise, to mark the place." (This is a very deceptive statement!)

Now you will distract The Spectator to take his attention off which part of the deck is which. You can do this by one of several means. I suggest that you turn to the previous page, where the picture of Penn & Teller is. As you show The Spectator the picture, you just point to the two faces, saying, "This is Penn, and this is Teller, and this is their card trick. It always works. There's a money-back guarantee!" Then you close the book, and turn back to the deck of cards.

Lift off the upper portion of the deck, which is lying across the lower part. Tell The Spectator to look at the card thus exposed. "Just look at the card you cut to in the deck." (By now, he's forgotten just how that cut was made, and he simply looks at your "force" card, the three of clubs.) When he has seen it, you hand him the rest of the deck and tell him to mix the cards thoroughly. He does that.

Now ask The Spectator to concentrate on his card. Look silly, as if you are picking something up by E.S.P. Say things like, "Clear your mind and don't think about hamburgers or atomic war." Some people will take you seriously!

Now reach into the deck and pull out any card, but peek at it first to be sure it's *not* the three of clubs, because you *want* to be wrong! Smiling, you announce, "This is your card, right?" as you show it. The answer will be NO! Try it again, two more times, and fail twice more, looking more and more annoyed. Try to look like a real phony psychic. Penn & Teller suggest that you should look as if you're trying to read the back of a cereal box located across the street. That's the way psychics usually look.

Then, apparently in desperation, turn to the index of this book (being careful not to show The Spectator the book's last few pages). Look up the heading "Tricks that go wrong: what to do." You'll be referred to page 161. Turn to that page and follow the instructions you find there, while The Spectator reads over your shoulder. Surprise!

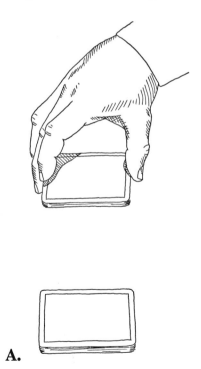

A.

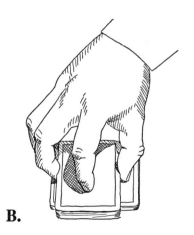

B.

DENNY LEE & MINH
U.S.A.

The motto of this spectacular team is, "We've mastered the impossible." Seeing their work, you just might believe that. With an impressive collection of stage scenery and props gathered over many years of traveling worldwide, the two can work in almost any circumstances, with a small person-to-person show or a large stage presentation. Young Alan Nguyen, whom you have already met in this book, often joins the team on stage. The beautiful Minh Dang is an indispensable part of the act.

Denny, at 17, was one of the youngest persons ever to graduate from the Chavez College of Magic in California. His active, exciting style has captivated audiences ever since. Whether he is escaping from a locked trunk, swallowing razor blades, vanishing from a box or performing the incredible levitation trick with Minh, he always seems to be rushing on to the next fascinating miracle.

Says Denny of the magic act, "No other form of show business commands such a powerful audience reaction. From ages 1 to 100, it's universal. There is no age barrier and no language barrier with creative feats of magic." Once you master the trick that Denny Lee & Minh offer you, I think you'll agree.

E.S.P. BY TELEPHONE
THE EFFECT:

The Wizard asks The Spectator to select freely any card from any deck of cards. The Spectator does and names the card. The Wizard then looks up the phone number of a friend who, he says, has the power to read minds. The Spectator himself dials the number given him, and simply asks the friend of The Wizard what card he is thinking of. The mysterious friend names it correctly!

HOW IT'S DONE:

Of course, to do this trick you'll need a good friend you can trust to keep the secret. Near his telephone, he must keep a copy of this list:

Alan .... Ace of Clubs	Elvis .... Ace of Hearts	James .... Ace of Spades	Peter .... Ace of Diamonds
Andy .... 2 of Clubs	Eric .... 2 of Hearts	John .... 2 of Spades	Phil .... 2 of Diamonds
Arthur .... 3 of Clubs	Eugene .... 3 of Hearts	Julius .... 3 of Spades	Pierre .... 3 of Diamonds
Barry .... 4 of Clubs	Frank .... 4 of Hearts	Lee .... 4 of Spades	Reggie .... 4 of Diamonds
Bill .... 5 of Clubs	Fred .... 5 of Hearts	Mark .... 5 of Spades	Richard .... 5 of Diamonds
Bob .... 6 of Clubs	Gary .... 6 of Hearts	Marvin .... 6 of Spades	Ronald .... 6 of Diamonds
Bruce .... 7 of Clubs	George .... 7 of Hearts	Max .... 7 of Spades	Sam .... 7 of Diamonds
Buddy .... 8 of Clubs	Harold .... 8 of Hearts	Mike .... 8 of Spades	Stan .... 8 of Diamonds
Calvin .... 9 of Clubs	Harry .... 9 of Hearts	Mitch .... 9 of Spades	Steve .... 9 of Diamonds
Charlie .... 10 of Clubs	Homer .... 10 of Hearts	Nathan .... 10 of Spades	Tom .... 10 of Diamonds
Claude .... Jack of Clubs	Howard .... Jack of Hearts	Neil .... Jack of Spades	Victor .... Jack of Diamonds
Danny .... Queen of Clubs	Hugh .... Queen of Hearts	Nick .... Queen of Spades	Walter. Queen of Diamonds
David .. .. King of Clubs	Jack .... King of Hearts	Paul .... King of Spades	Wilbur .. King of Diamonds

Or, if you prefer to call a female friend, you can use this list:

Alexis .... Ace of Clubs	Deborah .... Ace of Hearts	Jackie .... Ace of Spades	Maria ...... Ace of Diamonds
Alice .... 2 of Clubs	Diane .... 2 of Hearts	Jane .... 2 of Spades	Martha .... 2 of Diamonds
Angela .... 3 of Clubs	Donna .... 3 of Hearts	Judith .... 3 of Spades	Mary .... 3 of Diamonds
Anna .... 4 of Clubs	Doris .... 4 of Hearts	Judy .... 4 of Spades	May .... 4 of Diamonds
Audrey .... 5 of Clubs	Edith .... 5 of Hearts	Julia .... 5 of Spades	Michele ...... 5 of Diamonds
Betty .... 6 of Clubs	Eleanor .... 6 of Hearts	Kathy .... 6 of Spades	Muriel .... 6 of Diamonds
Blossom .... 7 of Clubs	Elizabeth .... 7 of Hearts	Laura .... 7 of Spades	Nicole .... 7 of Diamonds
Carol .... 8 of Clubs	Elsie .... 8 of Hearts	Leah .... 8 of Spades	Nina .... 8 of Diamonds
Catherine .... 9 of Clubs	Felicia .... 9 of Hearts	Lisa .... 9 of Spades	Renee .... 9 of Diamonds
Charlotte .... 10 of Clubs	Francis .... 10 of Hearts	Lucy .... 10 of Spades	Robyn .... 10 of Diamonds
Christine ...... Jack of Clubs	Greta .... Jack of Hearts	Lulu .... Jack of Spades	Rose ...... Jack of Diamonds
Claire .... Queen of Clubs	Heather .... Queen of Hearts	Maggie .... Queen of Spades	Ruth ... Queen of Diamonds
Daisy .... King of Clubs	Iris .... King of Hearts	Margaret .... King of Spades	Sally ..... King of Diamonds

You, of course, must also carry a duplicate of the list you prefer to use. Just before performing the trick, call up your friend and tell him (or her) to wait by the phone with a copy of the list all ready to be referred to.

When The Spectator chooses his card, you will learn what it is, and, pretending to look up your friend's name, you actually look up *the card that has been chosen*, and you note the first name listed opposite it. Then, supposing that The Spectator chose the five of clubs, you tell The Spectator to call your friend "Bill," (or "Audrey," if you use the second list) and you give him your friend's telephone number. As soon as your friend answers, he looks up the name that The Spectator asks for, and names the correct card! That's as close to E.S.P. as you can get!

TINA LENERT
U.S.A.

Combining mime and magic can be very entertaining, because the two disciplines are so similar. The mime uses body movement to give an illusion; the magician employs props and misdirection to accomplish the same effect. We might describe Tina Lenert as the Cinderella of Magic. With her raggy-looking character as a cleaning lady, complete with cart, broom, bucket and mop, this clever performer's possessions suddenly come to life and dance around with her. Of course, as in all good fairy tales, the ending is happy.

Tina is also a skilled musician. She started performing with a musical group, not suspecting that she would eventually branch off into performing street magic/mime and then move to stage and television work.

About her position as a female performer, she comments, "You might say that I am not a woman magician at all, since the magic in my act happens *to* me, and is actually performed by the coat and mop that represent a man!" She feels that women have not explored the possibilities of doing unique, new magical tricks that suit them better than the ones men have been doing for so many years.

Tina is married to a very well-known magician, Mike Caveney. He even helps her design parts of her performance. Mike has invented some clever routines for other magicians, and though the trick Tina offers you is not his invention, Tina and Mike are eager to share it with you.

THE EVAPORATING GLASS
THE EFFECT:

The Wizard shows The Spectator a small glass which is partially filled with liquid. He stands it on the palm of his left hand. Covering it with his right hand, he seals it between his two hands so it appears it can't get out. The Wizard slowly closes both palms together, then opens his hands to show that the glass — plus the liquid — has vanished! The Spectator is amazed!

HOW IT'S DONE:

Some tricks are especially effective because they involve objects and materials that seem impossible to manipulate. The prop for this trick is handy to have, and it will only cost about two dollars to make.

Look for a small glass, usually called a "whiskey glass." It should have straight, rather than sloping, sides. (See illustration A.) Now shop around and find a soft rubber ball that will plug snugly into the glass. The ball should just enter the glass with a bit of pressure, and seal the top tightly.

Prepare the ball by punching a hole through it with a thin screwdriver, from one side directly through the center to the other side. Through this hole, pass a piece of black elastic — which you can get anywhere sewing supplies are sold. It should be of medium thickness and about three feet long. Make a double knot in one end so that the elastic won't slip back out of the hole.

You must wear a jacket to perform this miracle. Fasten a large safety-pin to the inside back of your collar, where the label or small loop is. Pass the free end of the elastic through the end of the safety pin and pull it through until the rubber ball hangs about six inches above the bottom back edge of your jacket.

Put on the jacket and you are ready to perform. Until you have perfected this trick, practice it without liquid in the glass. With your jacket unbuttoned, and the rubber ball hanging out of sight inside the back of your jacket, pick up the glass with your right hand, and place it into your left hand. Now tell The Spectator that you have some "magic powder," and reach your right hand around to your back right-hand pocket. Bring out your hand as if you have a pinch of powder between your fingers, and drop the invisible powder into the glass.

"I think we need a bit more," you say, as you again reach around to your pocket. But *this* time, you will take hold of the rubber ball, grasping it as shown (see illustration B), and smoothly bring it up to the glass as if to drop in more "powder" into it. Your right hand will now cover the top of the glass, and your fingers will cover the glass from sight. Hold your hands close to your body, near the front edge of your jacket. Push the ball firmly into the glass with your palm, sealing the liquid inside. (See illustration C.)

Now you simply open your hands at the back, enough to let the glass slip through them. It will go inside the jacket and around to the back. If it stays up at the front, just lean forward a bit, and the glass will slide around to the back.

The glass is gone from your hands, but The Spectator doesn't know it — yet. Holding your hands in the same way, you bring them forward and away from your body. (See illustration D.) Hold that position for a few seconds, then slowly bring your palms together as if crushing the glass. Open your hands and show they are empty! Pull your sleeves up about six inches to show that the glass is not there. The Spectator will be quite astounded.

NOTES: Don't sit down right after doing this, because the glass will suddenly be in a very awkward position! Leave your jacket unbuttoned until you've removed the prop, or you will go around with a strange bump on your back. Make all your moves smoothly. Don't rush. This is a beautiful trick, and you don't want to waste its effect. And don't put too much liquid in the glass, or you'll get an eyeful!

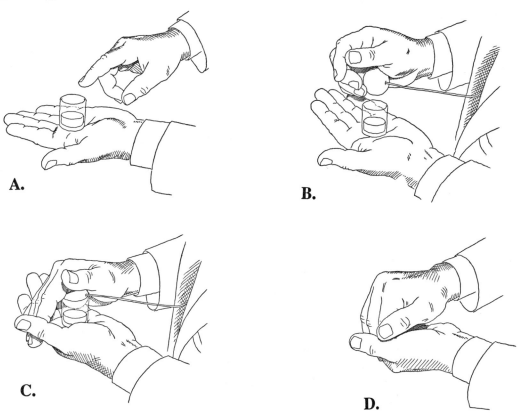

A.

B.

C.

D.

GOLDFINGER & DOVE
U.S.A.

In the years that I have known this couple, their act has undergone many changes. At first, Goldfinger wore the traditional tuxedo or tailcoat so favored by magicians. Then he changed his look completely by adopting bright, flashy costumes and very upbeat music. The act has developed and changed so much that now it's almost entirely new.

One thing hasn't changed, though. The performance uses a lot of color and special lighting to create a sense of humor and mystery. Goldfinger moves quickly and does more miracles per minute than you can count! Whether he is eating fire, producing showers of playing cards, or materializing birds out of thin air, this popular and artistic team is booked solidly for months, all around the world. They bring great fun and entertainment wherever they go.

Goldfinger and Dove share with you one of their favorite little puzzlers.

HOW MANY CARDS?
THE EFFECT:

The Wizard and The Spectator each cut off a number of cards from a shuffled deck. Each secretly counts his packet of cards, and The Wizard is able to tell The Spectator how many cards The Spectator has cut off! The trick is repeated twice more, and the third time, The Wizard is able to tell The Spectator how many cards he has, even before The Spectator has finished counting his cards!

HOW IT'S DONE:

This trick has actually fooled a lot of magicians because it's so simple. Invite The Spectator to cut a packet of cards from the top of the deck by saying, "Take off some cards, but not more than a quarter of the deck, please." You casually watch to see how many cards he takes, then you cut some off for yourself, *making sure to take at least 4 or 5 more than The Spectator did.* (You need only estimate — you don't have to know the exact number.) With a little practice, this will be easy.

Now each of you secretly counts your cards. Suppose you have 16 cards. You say, "I believe that I have the same number of cards that *you* have, plus *one* extra, plus enough to make *your* packet equal 15." (Of course, there's nothing special about the number 15 — the number you use may be different. The rule is: use a number that is one less than the number of cards you have counted into your own hand.)

Now ask The Spectator to count his cards and place them onto the table, one at a time, at the same time that you do. Together, you deal the cards onto the table, one at a time, into two separate piles, counting each card aloud as you set it down. You are secretly watching as The Spectator comes to his last card. Suppose that last card is number ten. As you both come to the tenth card, you emphasize the word, "ten!" and you pause. "And one extra," you say, putting one more down, "plus enough to make your hand equal 15. That will be 5." You count, "1,2,3,4,5," the remaining cards.

Immediately, you gather up the cards, and say, "Look! I'll do it again!" You give the cards a quick shuffle and repeat the trick. (Remember — cut off more than he does, count them, subtract one to get the new number, make your announcement using the new number, then count the cards as described.) Again, it works.

Here comes the big surprise. You offer to do it "one more time." But as you gather up the cards this time, you mentally add together the number of *his* cards and the number of *yours*. Remember this new number. Suppose it's 30. Bring the two packets together, and glance at the *bottom card* of this combined, larger packet. Suppose it is the jack of spades. This is now your "key" card. Drop the large packet face down on the rest of the cards.

Now you say to The Spectator, "This time, you can cut off almost half the deck, if you want to." He makes his cut, and you make yours, but you cut off only as many cards as you need to get the "key" card in your hand. Fan out your cards and pretend to count them, but instead, look through your fan of cards until you find the jack of spades. Starting at that key card, count silently to the left until you reach the last card in your fan. Suppose you count eight cards. Quickly subtract *that* number from 30. I *do* hope you got 22? (The Spectator has not even finished counting *his* cards yet!)

You immediately announce, "You have only twenty-two... Oops! Sorry, I was a bit too fast there!" Then, as The Spectator finishes counting his cards and discovers that he *does* have twenty-two, you toss your cards down and remark, "I guess I was too quick!"

ANGEL
U.S.A.

Angel has made music a big part of his act. In fact, his four-piece rock music group, known as Chris Angel, performs every minute he is on stage. He's not the kind of magician who can put on his show in a small room! The elaborate special effects in this act represent cutting-edge technology. Smoke, lights and strobe flashes fill the theater when Angel is working.

The importance of music in Angel's current stage act may have something to do with his early interests. As a six-year-old, he began learning to play the drums. He entered the modeling profession soon after, traveling with various companies and taking prizes for his work. Then he spent two years studying acting in New York, and appeared in several movies. He developed an interest in magic very early, and has competed in contests all over the world. Today, with his brother George, a songwriter and producer, he works to improve his 30-minute stage spectacle for television and commercial shows.

His most effective illusion is a classic one called The Metamorphosis, in which one person is switched for another at breathtaking speed. You'll be happy to learn that the trick Angel has for you doesn't require clouds of smoke or bursts of flame. But it is a real surprise!

THE GHOST PENCIL

THE EFFECT:

The Wizard says he will make his signature appear magically on a business card. He places the business card on his left hand and slowly brings the point of a short pencil down against the card three times. By the third time, The Spectator finds that the pencil is gone, yet the signature has appeared on the other side of the card!

HOW IT'S DONE:

The prop is very easy to make. You'll need about a dozen business cards, a wide rubber band, and a short wooden pencil. Take one of the business cards and cut it exactly in half, as shown. (See illustration A.) Stack the others together, and place the rubber band around the stack, after writing your name, in pencil, on the left side of the front of the top card. Now place the cut-off left side of the card under the rubber band so it appears to be part of the top card you've written on. Put the packet in your left pocket, the short pencil in your right.

Stand to the right of The Spectator as you perform the trick. Take out the packet of cards and tell him, "This is my magical business card." You indicate the name and address printed on the top card; say, "I'll make my signature appear on the card, by magic." Holding the false half-card in place against the packet, pull the top card by the right hand end, out from under the rubber band and turn it over, face down. (See illustrations B and C.) Place the packet of business cards in your left pocket with your left hand, and then place the single card, *face down*, onto your left palm.

Taking the short pencil from your pocket with your right hand, hold it as if to write. (See illustration D.) Tell The Spectator to watch the card carefully. Point the pencil at the card and touch the card with it, counting, "One!" Slowly bring the pencil up near your right ear, then back down again to touch the card, counting, "Two!" Bring the pencil back up to the ear, but this time stick the pencil into your collar at the back of your neck. (See illustration E.) Your empty right hand, still held in a writing position, comes back down to the card with the same rhythm. (See illustration F.)

"Uh-oh!" you say "That pencil has a way of disappearing just when I'm ready to do this miracle. But maybe it worked anyway. Let's see." You turn the card over, and The Spectator sees your name written there, but the pencil has become a ghost. . .

This is a great way to get The Spectator to walk away with your business card!

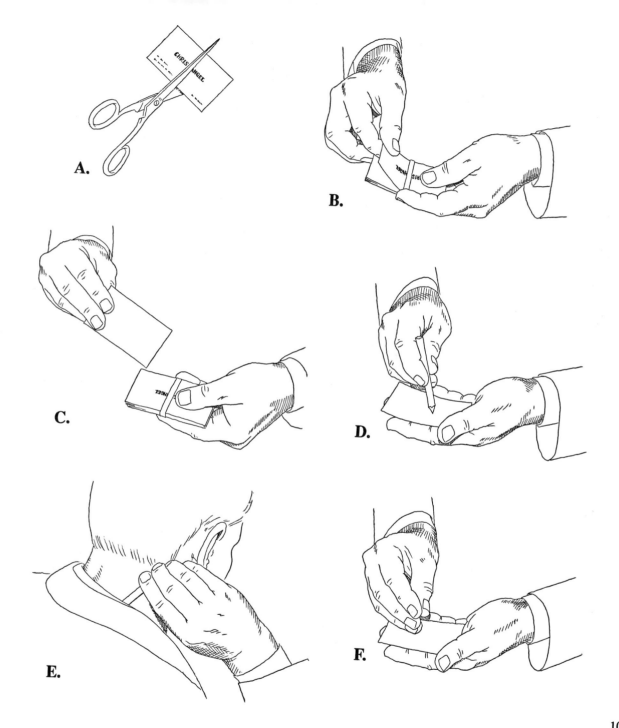

A.

B.

C.

D.

E.

F.

TONY ALBANO
U.S.A.

Tony Albano is a popular entertainer on cruise lines, traveling all over the world and working his wizardry to the great delight of the passengers. While on land, he has performed at amusement parks, on television and in theaters with his fast-moving show. His bride Julie has recently joined the act.

Tony started his career as a Wizard by working in school shows in his native Pennsylvania. He did so well with children's shows that he was asked to serve as the resident artist at a popular New York magic club. He then graduated to television and the cruise lines. When working for a "captive" audience, a magician must have a large repertoire, since he may be entertaining that same group for weeks on end! But Tony and Julie manage to do that quite well.

Tony hopes you will enjoy this trick.

TIME FOR E.S.P.

THE EFFECT:

A few different issues of TIME (or NEWSWEEK, or a similar magazine) are offered to The Spectator by The Wizard. The Spectator chooses one, names a page number, and turns to that page. He is asked to look at any prominent illustration on that page, then to close the magazine. The Wizard is able to reproduce the illustration and even write down some of the caption or accompanying title, without handling the chosen magazine.

HOW IT'S DONE:

You'll have to go around to a few friends to get some duplicate copies of the magazine you'll be using. You can get (a) six of the same issue, or (b) pairs of three issues. In either case, you must also get five additional different *covers* that will fit over these magazines. Carefully open the staples in the center fold of five of the copies, then slip the staples out. Substitute the covers, so you will now have either (a) six magazines that are the same *inside* but have different covers, or (b) three pairs of magazines, with three sets of insides but with six different covers.

Offer The Spectator the magazine of his choice. Casually, you also pick one up. In the case of (a) above, any other magazine will be alright for you to pick up. In the case of (b), you must pick up the "twin" of the one The Spectator chose. Of course, he thinks you have an entirely different magazine in your hand.

Ask The Spectator to name a number between, say, one and sixty. Ask him to turn to that page, and demonstrate with your magazine how you want him to hold it — right in front of his face, so you cannot see his page. Secretly, you are turning to that same page in your copy of the magazine. Simply glance at it, noting a prominent feature of the page. Then close your copy.

Tell The Spectator to think of whatever he sees on his chosen page. Then he is to close the magazine and keep it in his hands. Take a pad of paper, and without letting The Spectator see what you are writing or drawing, put down a representation of what you remember seeing when you looked into your magazine. You can tell The Spectator that you are having a hard time "getting" what he is thinking, and ask him to take another quick look at it. As soon as he sees it the second time, you exclaim, "Ah! I wondered what that was!" and you rapidly scribble something on your pad.

Ask The Spectator what he saw on the chosen page, then show him what you have drawn on your pad. The Spectator will be *amazed*!

ARTHUR BENJAMIN
U.S.A.

Magicians are as varied as the tricks they perform. I'm sure you're convinced of that by now, having met all the interesting folks in this book. Art Benjamin, however, has one ability that is extremely rare. He can multiply large numbers together — in his head — faster than you can enter them into a calculator! He squares and divides extremely large numbers at great speed, and in general plays with figures as easily as you eat a bowl of corn flakes.

Scientists have studied this ability and are coming up with some answers; however, much of what the "savants" do is still a mystery. When Arthur performs, magicians and scientists go away shaking their heads in amazement. It's all very logical and Arthur delights in giving you an explanation, if you ask! Most of his act is genuine, the result of an unusual ability. However, Arthur does use some secret number tricks when he performs.

Right now, at Harvey Mudd College, in California, Arthur is known as "Professor." He teaches mathematics at this prestigious school. Here, in our book, Professor Benjamin shares one of his secrets with you. It is based upon a simple mathematical idea, but has a great twist at the end!

GOTCHA!
THE EFFECT:

The Wizard hands The Spectator a pencil and a card with this pattern on it:

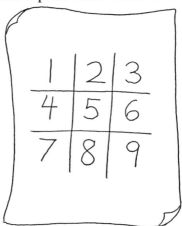

He then takes some coins from his pocket, counts out a number of them, hiding them from The Spectator, and closes them in his fist. He tells The Spectator, "Here in my hand I have the same number of coins as the number you're about to arrive at." The Spectator is told to select three of the numbers written on the card. He adds those three numbers together, and The Wizard tells him to divide the total in half. The Spectator laughs, saying that it can't be done, because the added number is 15! But The Wizard tells him it *can* be done, and proves it. When he opens his hand, he shows The Spectator *seven and a half coins*!

HOW IT'S DONE:

Ready for the secret? First, take a regular penny and cut it exactly in half with a hacksaw. (If you're uncomfortable working with tools or are too young to do so, enlist the aid of an experienced helper who can keep your secret.) Finish the edges with a file so it's nice and smooth. Keep that in your pocket with seven other pennies. When you go for the coins in your pocket, you take out the seven pennies plus the half coin.

The instructions to The Spectator for choosing the number are really easy. Tell him to circle any one of the numbers on the card, then cross out both rows (across and up-and-down) in which that number occurs. Next, he is to circle any other uncrossed number, and cross out the two rows, in the same way as before. This always leaves just one number, which he is told to circle also. When he adds these three circled numbers together, he *always gets 15*!

Now, when he's told to "take exactly half of that number," he laughs, of course. But when The Wizard insists, he gets seven and a half, and The Wizard merely opens his hand to confound The Spectator who thought he couldn't possibly be right!

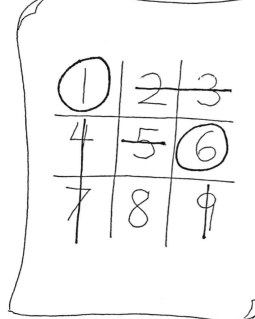

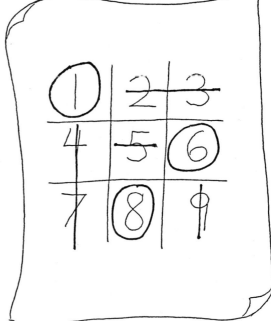

STEVE SHAW
South Africa

S teve Shaw is a mentalist. That means that he does tricks that seem to be performed through E.S.P., clairvoyance and prediction abilities. Sometimes people think Steve really has psychic powers, and he has a hard time convincing them that he's only a performer. Steve, who has appeared on numerous TV shows, has also done everything from catching a bullet in his teeth to being buried alive and escaping from six feet under ground.

A few years ago, Steve and his colleague, Michael Edwards, showed how easily some scientists could be fooled into believing in psychic powers. The magicians were tested at a famous university, and convinced the scientists they could do real magic. When the magicians finally revealed the tricks they had used, the scientists were quite surprised, to say the least!

Here's a trick that Steve Shaw wants you to have. You'll always be able to do it as long as you have 17¢ in your pocket!

I NEVER MISS!

THE EFFECT:

The Wizard places three coins — a dime, a nickel and a penny — on the table before The Spectator. He is holding another coin in his closed hand, but he doesn't show it to The Spectator yet. He tells The Spectator that he'll only do the trick once, but he is sure his prediction will be right. Then he asks The Spectator to choose any one of the three coins. No matter what The Spectator does, The Wizard ends up having the same coin!

HOW IT'S DONE:

Lay the three different coins out on the table. You will hold a fourth coin, a penny, in your closed hand. Say to The Spectator, "Now I will only do this once, but I'm *positive* that my prediction will be right. I want you to do this quickly, without hesitation. Ready? OK, just reach down there, pick up any *two* coins and hand them to me. Quickly!"

The Spectator does this. Now the trick can proceed in a number of different ways. We'll discuss each one in order.

First, suppose The Spectator picks up the dime and nickel. He hands them to you and you put them away again in your pocket. That leaves the penny on the table. You ask him to cover the penny with his hand, and you place your hand beside his in a similar position. Then you ask him to take his hand away, you do the same, and he sees the two pennies side-by-side on the table. Your prediction was correct!

Second, suppose The Spectator picks up the penny and nickel and hands them to you. You tell him, "OK, now choose *one* of those coins. Quick!" Suppose The Spectator chooses the penny. You tell him, "Right! Now close your fist on it, and bring it up against *my* fist." You tell him to slowly open his fist, and you open yours at the same time. You are both holding pennies, and your prediction is right!

If The Spectator should choose the nickel, you take the nickel from him, and sweep the dime on the table and the nickel back into your pocket. Tell him, "Right! Now close your fist again. You're not going to believe this! Open your hand at the same time I do." As you both open your hands, The Spectator sees you both have pennies. Your prediction is correct!

(If The Spectator has picked up the penny and the dime, just substitute "dime" for "nickel" and "nickel" for "dime" in the above two paragraphs, and again, your prediction will be right!)

It sounds complicated, but it's really easy once you practice it a few times. You'll catch on fast, I'm sure, and you'll have another trick that you can always have ready to demonstrate.

JAMES RANDI
U.S.A.

The time has come for me to contribute one of my favorite tricks to this book. First, I must tell you something about myself.

I'm a very lucky person who, as a youngster born and raised in Toronto, Canada, managed to meet some friendly, helpful people who practiced the art of magic. They accepted me as one of them and they helped me develop my skills until I was able to enter the field professionally. Along the way, I read many, many books about magic and magicians that offered me help and encouragement.

If this book, which features some of my magician friends, has given you a few interesting tricks to do for *your* friends, I will be very pleased. The fun, insight and camaraderie that magic can bring make it one of the most interesting of all hobbies. I am delighted to have been able to introduce you to some of those ideas, so generously offered by my friends.

I hope that I have deserved at least some of the honors that have been given me. I can tell you that, quite honestly, one of the greatest honors that ever comes my way is a round of applause from a satisfied audience. It is my ultimate reward.

That's enough about me. Let's get to work on this next tricky bit of business, shall we?

CARDS IN THE POCKET
THE EFFECT:

The Wizard removes a deck of cards from its box, cuts it a couple of times, and places it face down on the table. The Spectator also cuts it a few times, then picks it up and places it behind his back. The Wizard asks him to cut it once more, out of sight behind his back, then to remove the top card without looking at it and slide it into his (The Spectator's) right-hand pocket. He is then asked to take the bottom card, again without looking at it, and place it in his left-hand pocket.

The Wizard thinks a bit, then announces the two cards!

HOW IT'S DONE:

First, you have secretly arranged your deck of cards in order before you sealed it away in its box. In order to do so, and to remember how you "stacked" your deck of cards, you will have to memorize a silly rhyming sentence, one that has been known to magicians for a long, long time. It is:

EIGHT KINGS THREATENED TO SAVE
NINETY-FIVE QUEENS FOR ONE SICK KNAVE.

Here's what it means: eight, king, three, ten, two, seven, nine, five, queen, four, ace, six, jack. (A jack is also known as a knave.) If I repeat the special sentence, placing the card names beneath the important parts, I think you'll see what I mean:

EIGHT KINGS THREATENED TO SAVE
8   K   3   10 2   7

NINETY-FIVE QUEENS FOR ONE SICK KNAVE
9   5   Q   4   A   6   J

Get it? OK, now memorize this word: CHaSeD. You now have the order of the suits — Clubs, Hearts, Spades, Diamonds — as you will use them.

Now we're ready to "stack," or arrange, our deck of cards. Start with the eight of clubs, placing it face up on the table. Place the king of hearts, also face up, on top of it, continuing with the three of spades. Do you see what we're doing? We are arranging the deck in a special order, the numbers being governed by the rhyming sentence, and the suits by the special word.

Just so you'll be sure, here's the complete order of the deck, from the top down:

8C, KH, 3S, 10D, 2C, 7H, 9S, 5D, QC, 4H, AS, 6D, JC, 8H, KS, 3D, 10C, 2H, 7S, 9D, 5C, QH, 4S, AD, 6C, JH, 8S, KD, 3C, 10H, 2S, 7D, 9C, 5H, QS, 4D, AC, 6H, JS, 8D, KC, 3H, 10S, 2D, 7C, 9H, 5S, QD, 4C, AH, 6S, JD.

With this stacked deck in its box, you're ready to perform. Remove the deck, and cut it several times, carefully. If you think about it, you'll see that cutting it only changes the place where the deck *begins*, but it doesn't change the *order* at all! Thus, if you know the *bottom* card on that deck, you also know the *top* card.

For example, suppose the bottom card is the two of hearts. No, you don't have to peek at the list printed above! Just think of the memorized sentence and the memorized word. Eight kings threatened to — ah! there's the "two" you're looking for, and following it is the word "save," which we know stands for "seven." So the next card (it's on the top now, of course) is a seven. And let's see, in the word "CHASED," the important letter that follows the "H" for "hearts" is "S" for "spades." So the top card is the seven of spades!

Here's how we use this idea: You instruct The Spectator to cut the deck behind his back. Then he is told to remove the top card and put it in his left pocket (pants or jacket) without looking at it. Next, he is to remove the bottom card and place it in his right pocket. Now, he doesn't know what cards he's put away. Nor do you — but you're about to find out.

You pick up the remainder of the deck, and simply glance at the bottom card on it while you remark to The Spectator that if you looked through the entire deck, you'd be able to tell him for sure what cards he has, but you're going to do it the hard way — by magic. Knowing the bottom card on the remainder of the deck, you figure out what the next card would be, according to our system above, and you know that it is the one in his *right* pocket. (Trust me, that's correct.) And, the card following *that* one is the card in his *left* pocket!

The way you reveal this to him can be very dramatic. Here's what I suggest. Suppose that you have seen the five of hearts on the bottom of the deck as you picked it up. Say to The Spectator, "I believe that you have the queen of spades and the four of diamonds. But I'll give you a choice. Would you like to have the queen in your right pocket and the four in your left, or do you prefer to have the four in your right and the queen in your left? It's up to you!" The Spectator may say that he wants it the first way, and since you know that is the way it actually is, you say to him, "OK, you're the boss. Remove the queen of spades from your right pocket, sir, and the four of diamonds from your left pocket!" The Spectator does so, and you're a big hero!

Ah, but what if The Spectator decides he wants it the other way around? Are you stuck? Not at all! You simply give him one chance to change his mind. If he doesn't, you announce, "Gee, I'm sorry, sir. You'll find that *you're* wrong, and *I'm* right. You have the queen in your *right* pocket and the four in your *left*. Look and you'll see!" At that point, just be sure The Spectator isn't bigger than you!

Well, that's it for now. My magical friends and I hope that you will carefully practice the tricks described in this book, and that you'll have a lot of enjoyment from performing them once you've rehearsed them thoroughly. Just remember that it's all in fun, and missing a trick is only a minor disaster — it's not the end of the world! Finding out how the human mind works can be fascinating, and one way to find out is by setting out to fool someone. In doing so, I hope that you may also learn that you, too, can be deceived.

Enjoy your adventure in magic!

James "The Amazing" Randi
Plantation, Florida

The Props

Tricks that use a deck of cards

Tricks that use a
deck of cards
(CONTINUED)

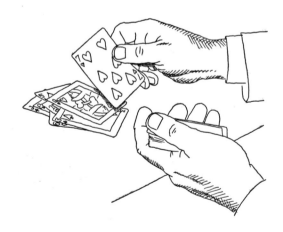

Tricks that use coins

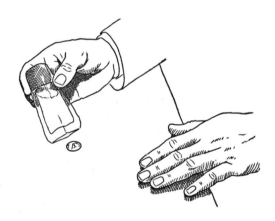

Tricks that use paper

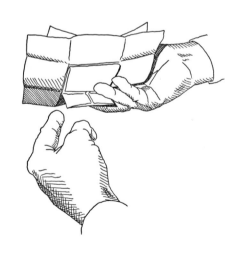

Tricks that use a handkerchief or napkin

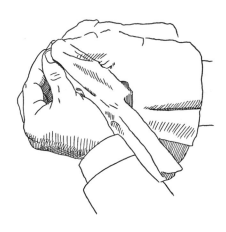

Tricks that use string or a shoelace

Restored String (page 44)
Vanishing Knot, Is It Not? (page 40)

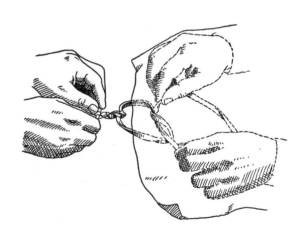

Tricks that use this book

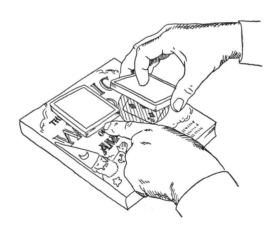

Trick that uses magazines

Tricks that use pencils or crayons

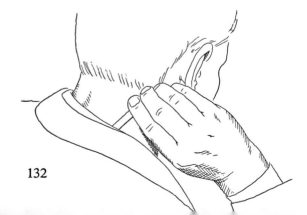

Trick that uses a glass

Tricks that use a rubber band

Organizations of Interest to Budding Wizards

Abbott's Magic Company
Colon, MI 49040
USA

❧

Flosso/Hornmann Magic Shop
45 West 34th Street
New York City, NY 10001
USA

Genii Magazine
P. O. Box 36068
Los Angeles, CA 90036
USA

◈

International Brotherhood of Magicians
103 North Main Street
Bluffton, OH 45817-0089
USA

◈

The Magic Circle
13 Calder Avenue
Brookmans Park
Herts AL9 7AH
ENGLAND

Magicus Journal
Lagarrigue, 81109 Castres
FRANCE

❧

Magirama
Caixa Postal 746-ZC-OO
20,000 Rio de Janeiro-RJ
BRAZIL

❧

Society of American Magicians
P. O. Box 368
Mango, FL 34262-0368
USA

Society of Young Magicians
P.O. Box 375
Nashua, NH 03061
USA

಄

Stevens Magic Emporium
3238 E. Douglas
Wichita, KS 67208
USA

಄

Supreme Magic Company
64 High Street
Bideford, Devon EX39 2AN
ENGLAND

Tannen's Magic Shop &
The Magic Manuscript
6 West 32nd Street
New York, NY 10001-3808
USA

Glossary

An act

A performer such as a magician, with or without assistants. Also refers to the actual performance as seen by the audience.

To complete the cut

To place a cut-off portion of cards under the deck and square up the deck.

To cut

With cards, to lift off a portion of them.

To deal
To take cards, one at a time, from the top of the deck. A deal can be performed "face down," as usually seen, or "face up."

A deck of cards
An entire set of 52 cards, sometimes plus a Joker or two.

Effect
The final result of The Wizard's performance.

Escape act
An act that consists of freeing oneself from bonds, manacles, etc.; the act perfected by Harry Houdini.

Face down

In cards, with the deck positioned so that the backs are facing up and the faces are down.

Face up

In cards, with the deck positioned so the faces are up and the backs are down.

Gaff

A secret method of applying trickery. Putting glue on the ends of a piece of string to hold them together would be considered a gaff.

Gimmick

A special piece of equipment or a prepared object used by the Wizard. A prepared loop of string with two ends secretly glued together would be considered a gimmick.

Key card

A special, marked, or noted card, usually used to locate another card.

Mentalism

A type of magic in which The Wizard appears to use only mental powers to accomplish an effect.

Misdirection

Any means used by The Wizard to take the attention of The Spectator away from a crucial move.

A packet

A number of cards, not a complete deck, held together in one group.

To palm

To conceal something in the hand, secretly.

To produce

To cause something to appear as if by magic.

Prop

Any piece of equipment used by The Wizard. It may or may not be an ordinary object or substance.

To replace the cut

With cards, to replace a cut-off portion of cards into the deck.

The Spectator

The person viewing the trick.

To shuffle

To mix up a deck or packet of cards. A "riffle" shuffle, in which the cards are mixed by interleaving them, is much better than an "overhand" shuffle, where cards are merely shifted by sliding small packets over each other.

To steal

To pick something up, often from a secret place, unseen by the Spectator.

Trick

A performance by The Wizard that appears to be the result of strange powers.

The Wizard

The person performing the trick. YOU!

Index

EMERGENCY SECTION

Wherein Penn & Teller save your wretched skin
when a trick has gone wrong.

DO NOT TURN THIS PAGE!

The following section is for emergency use only. It may be used only ONCE, as it involves special printing ink that is ruined once it is exposed to light.

INSTRUCTIONS

If a card trick has gone wrong and you are looking very bad, follow these steps:

1. Recite this confession: I DIDN'T PRACTICE MY PERFORMANCE, SO IT DIDN'T WORK. I THOUGHT I HAD PSYCHIC POWERS, AND I MESSED UP. FROM NOW ON, I'LL DO IT USING TRICKERY. PSYCHIC POWERS ARE FOR FAIRY STORIES. I'VE LEARNED MY LESSON.

2. Turn the page.

HERE, "WIZARD". IS THIS THE CARD? THE Three OF Clubs ? 6

NOW GO TO YOUR ROOM AND PRACTICE! NEXT TIME YOU'RE ON YOUR OWN

—Penn & Teller

How did I get here?

Only
_____
knows for sure!